ISABELLA ROSSELLINI

ISABELLA ROSSELLINI

Quiet Renegade

CATHLEEN YOUNG

ST. MARTIN'S PRESS • NEW YORK

A 2M Communications Ltd. Production

Photo Research by Amanda Rubin

Design by Holly Block

Library of Congress Cataloging-in-Publication Data

Young, Cathleen.
 Isabella Rossellini.
  1. Rossellini, Isabella. 2. Motion picture actors
and actresses—United States—Biography. 3. Models,
Fashion—United States—Biography. I. Title.
PN2287.R7584Y6 1989 791.43'028'0924 [B] 88-30626
ISBN 0-312-02591-2

First Edition

10 9 8 7 6 5 4 3 2 1

For Lee,
a delight and inspiration
to all who know her.

ACKNOWLEDGMENTS

Special thanks to John Bailey, Bill Borden, Sue Jett, Nancy King, Patricia Knop, Mary Lambert, Steve Previn, and Tina Rathborne for granting interviews and sharing with me their universal respect and admiration for Isabella as well as their anecdotes. Lastly, I want to thank Madeleine Morel and Toni Lopopolo for their expertise, their patience, and their pivotal roles in making this book happen.

Contents

ISABELLA ROSSELLINI

PROLOGUE

Born in Rome just seconds before her twin sister on June 18, 1952, Isabella Fiorella Elettra Giovanna Rossellini came into the world amidst much fanfare as the Italian paparazzi—a particularly ferocious breed of freelancing, freewheeling hustlers who marauded with their cameras— tried desperately to photograph her newborn face. Her mother was Ingrid Bergman, a "fallen" goddess; her father, Roberto Rossellini, a mere mortal striving for artistic greatness, who, out of love, had dared to snatch Ingrid from Olympus.

The affair of Isabella's parents had unleashed an international torrent of ill will toward the two lovers. When Isabella was born, Ingrid was still an exile from America. Her mother's passionate love affair with the Italian film director, Roberto, the instrument of Isabella's own creation, was dying out, replaced by their unhappy marriage, which crumbled irrevocably day by day.

Isabella grew up in the shadow of a once-great love, her childhood spent living behind a facade of wealth and fame. In truth, with Ingrid's film career on the rocks and Roberto's efforts at directing proving fruitless, the family was little more than a traveling show. Ensconced in an old

Rolls Royce, they moved from town to town all over Europe, allowing small audiences to enjoy live performances from the former Hollywood star.

Perhaps because of the failure of the Rossellinis' careers, perhaps because their vision of great love could not withstand the hardships of reality, the marriage of Isabella's parents came apart. There was a messy divorce, a custody battle. That was followed by Isabella's life-threatening operation to save her from becoming possibly crippled or deformed by scoliosis. Later in Isabella's life, there were successes in broadcast journalism, the almost accidental success of becoming a top international model, and then the success, by design, of becoming a respected actress—a respect she did not begin earning until she emerged from the long shadows cast by her mother and father.

Today, Isabella Rossellini is poised on the threshold of greatness as an actress. At the age of thirty-six, she is standing in her own light, her luminous face reflecting light from the silver screen, much as her mother's did in her many films. The shadow of her parents' love is still there, but far behind her now.

CHAPTER

1

A WAY OUT

The Blue Lady is tired. Her hair smells like cigarette smoke from singing songs all night at the Slow Club. The thought of facing another lonely, tortured night fills her with despair. Her shoulders slump, punctuating her weariness. Her body has changed since the birth of little Donny. Now she has lovely rounded curves. *Frank can't get enough of me,* she thinks, then curses herself for having such a thought, but the thought lingers, snagged, as if by barbed wire. The phone rings.

It's him.

She hears the voice of her husband and then her son. She cries out. Then Frank is back. He's coming over.

She falls to the floor, her skin a shocking white against the dull red of the walls. She pulls a family portrait from underneath the couch. They seem so far away. But she will go on for them, her husband and son. She pulls off her wig. Her hair is pressed flat against her skull. She changes into her blue velvet robe, unaware of the man hiding in the closet, watching her every move.

Dorothy waits, occasionally glancing at the front door Frank will soon walk through and . . .

. . . No. She doesn't want to think about that yet because . . .

. . . Because someone is in her closet! Don't panic. Don't let him know you've spotted him. She grabs a huge carving knife in the kitchen. The gleam of the metal reassures her.

"What are you doing? Who are you? What's your name? What's your name?"

He won't say his name. He's playing with her. Her rage explodes.

She orders him to get undressed. The knife is poised at his groin as she kisses the sinews of his young body. He likes it.

"Don't look at me!" she screams.

The door. Frank is at the door.

Dorothy hides Jeffrey in the closet. She begs him to be quiet. Or else he will die. She moves to the door, opens it. A common-looking man enters.

"Shut up. It's Daddy, you shithead. Where's my bourbon?" Frank sits on the couch, perched on the edge, ready to attack. Silent and afraid, Dorothy moves around the room, trying not to let him see her cower. She hands Frank his drink, then lights a candle and pulls a chair into the middle of the room. She sits. Waiting.

"Spread your legs. Wider," Frank says. He slips to the floor. He pulls out a plastic oxygen mask, inhaling deeply. The drug frees him. She looks at him. He screams, telling her not to look at him. He hits her. She smiles.

"Baby wants blue velvet," he says. She stuffs the blue velvet sash of her robe into his mouth. He moans. He pulls her to the floor. He stuffs blue velvet into her mouth. She looks at him.

"Don't look at me," he screams. Out of the corner of her eye, she watches him, only a little afraid. She knows he's not dangerous anymore.

He stands over her. She waits for him to leave. When he does, Jeffrey slips out of the closet. She starts when he touches her. He helps her to the couch. He holds her. She guides his hand to her breast.

He touches her. He can't resist.

"Feel me," she says. "Hit me."

He pulls away from her and she slams her fist into the wall.

"Hit me! Hit me! Hit me!"

But she frightens him. He leaves.

"Help me," she whispers, but he cannot hear her.

Isabella Rossellini has the large dark eyes of a child not quite tough enough for the real world. Yet they are the eyes of a survivor, of a woman who is no stranger to pain and heartbreak, but who chooses to live surrounded by love and resounding laughter. She has an almost boyish face, a short, gamine haircut, and a chipped front tooth. But the impression lasts only for a second. The light changes and the boyishness is gone—disappearing like ephemera—and a different Isabella emerges, a woman who looks uncannily like her mother. The daughter has Ingrid's same big, wondering eyes, her high cheekbones and full, sensuous mouth. Even Isabella's voice, husky with overtones of hidden passions, reminds us of her heritage.

Like her mother, Isabella loves the process of creating a character and letting that character take over. Like her father, Isabella loves taking risks. Roberto Rossellini was not afraid of the dark side of human nature. He loved to explore—regardless of the consequences—what others preferred to keep hidden.

She grew up behind the camera, peering over her father's shoulder, hanging around the sets of her mother's movies. When Isabella finally took her place in front of the camera, she did so with a vengeance, baring her soul in every frame of *Blue Velvet*. We see Dorothy's obsessions, her fears, her vulnerabilities, her hatred, and, ultimately, her love. The emotional strain of making the movie almost gave her a nervous breakdown. To make it real, Isabella Rossellini, as her mother had done so many times before, dug deep inside herself to bring her character to life. Like mother, like daughter, but that is where the similarity ends.

Ingrid Bergman made a name for herself by becoming no less than a goddess in the minds of her fans, always portraying heroines who approached moral perfection. She became an idol, personifying goodness in films like *Intermezzo, For Whom the Bell Tolls, The Bells of St. Mary's, Notorious,* and *Casablanca*. Isabella Rossellini has already traveled light-years away from the screen world of radiant purity her famous mother inhabited.

Isabella has made a name for herself by revealing the dark side of human nature, nearly always portraying women with dark secrets, women filled with rage, women with strange sexual appetites, women on the edge, such as Madeleine in *Tough Guys Don't Dance* and Marie in *Siesta*. Her portrayal of Dorothy Vallens marked a stunning break with the sensibilities of her mother.

Ingrid Bergman never came to inhabit a character like Dorothy. One suspects, however, that she probably had some insight into the darker side of human nature.

"I cannot understand why people think I'm pure and full of nobleness," Ingrid said in her twenties. "Every human being has shadings of good and bad."

Isabella saw her mother trapped in the role of icon and wanted none of it. She has steadfastly sought controversial, complex roles. The role of Dorothy garnered Isabella more attention than she ever dreamed possible. And more criticism. Roger Ebert, film movie critic of the *Chicago Sun-Times*, railed against the film on "The Tonight Show" shortly after its release. Even the national syndicated film critic and columnist Rex Reed voiced the opinion that Isabella's mother "must be turning over in her grave." For Hollywood's newest star, reading these reviews was like watching strangers beat your child, the child being *Blue Velvet*, an unusual labor of love.

"This film is a trip into darkness and back out again," David Lynch, the director and writer of the film, told Jack Mathews in the September 26 issue of *The Los Angeles Times*.

He's right. And it's quite a trip.

David Lynch is not at all what you might expect. *Blue Velvet* is such a strange anomaly of hyperrealism and charged eroticism that you would expect its director to be a genius waif, or perhaps a tortured painter turned filmmaker sporting dark circles under weary eyes. In reality, Lynch looks, and seems, as American as apple pie, with hair the color of honey and changeable blue eyes. Lynch usually wears white Oxford shirts and baggy pleated pants. His collars have to be turned just so. He would look perfectly at home as a graduate student at any Ivy League college.

"There are things lurking in the world and within us that we have to deal with," reasons the youthful director. "You can evade them for awhile, for a long time, maybe, but if you face them and name them, they start losing their power. Once you name the enemy, you can deal with it a lot better."

Exactly what is the enemy in a film that people love to hate and hate to love?

"David is obsessed with obsession," Isabella told Stephen Schiff in the March 1987 issue of *Vanity Fair*. "He finds it irresistibly funny. He finds Frank comical in *Blue Velvet*, because Frank is so obsessed—even when Frank is raping me. When we were filming it, David couldn't stop laughing. He had to grab ahold of himself not to disturb the scene."

It all began with the romantic ballad "Blue Velvet," a song that Bobby Vinton crooned into a chart-topper in 1963. Lynch wanted to make a movie with the same title because the song, to him, evoked a rich atmosphere.

"The song comes from a certain time and brings with it feelings from that time," he explains. "So much of *Blue Velvet* the film has to do with this innocence and this naive sort of feeling from the fifties and the early sixties before horrors start bobbing up."

As Lynch speaks, his voice gains intensity. He has the enthusiasm, the cadences of a young boy—his words rush, then lull, then pour out in another rush of ideas. As his films show, he has never lost his wonder at the ways of the world.

"And I guess the next idea I got, which was more of a desire, was to sneak into a girl's room and watch her all night. And then while I was in there I would see something that would be a clue—maybe I wouldn't even realize it at the time—but maybe later I would know that was a clue to a mystery."

It's no mystery why *Blue Velvet* was hailed by the critics at the prestigious Cannes Film Festival as the work of a genius. The movie resonates with issues and subtexts rarely glimpsed in American filmmaking. *Blue Velvet* starts out deceptively simply. Lured in with the blissful idyll of the opening scene, the audience is engaged before the ensuing turbulence begins.

The sky is a sapphire blue and nearly every house in Lumberton sports a well-trimmed green lawn, a pristine white picket fence. Jeffrey's father waters his manicured lawn on this perfect day. Life seems good, orderly. Suddenly, Jeffrey's dad grabs the back of his head and falls to the ground, the hose still in his hand. Suddenly, the camera moves down, into the ground, where teeming beetles and ants fight to the death.

Jeffrey's father is hospitalized with a stroke. After a bedside reunion of father and son, Jeffrey spots a severed human ear while walking through a field he's passed through uneventfully hundreds of times before.

The ear is covered with fighting ants.

Jeffrey, good boy that he is, takes the ear to the police. But he can't get the ear—or the mystery surrounding it—out of his mind. Later that night, he pays a visit to a police detective, who kindly but firmly warns him to forget he ever saw the ear. Naturally, this piques Jeffrey's interest. Sandy, the detective's daughter, further encourages Jeffrey by telling him the few clues she's managed to pick up. Her dad has been investigating a case involving a woman named Dorothy Vallens who lives in the Deep River Apartments.

And, Sandy confides, a murder may be involved.

Posing as a bug exterminator, Jeffrey enters Dorothy's apartment and steals an extra set of keys hidden in the kitchen. Later that night, he sneaks back to search for more clues. When Dorothy returns unexpectedly, Jeffrey hides in the closet, spying on the lushly beautiful Dorothy as she undresses. Jeffrey spies on Dorothy and Frank, as they proceed to engage in a bizarre, cruel rape, though Dorothy seems to take a perverse pleasure in her victimization.

Jeffrey imagines himself Dorothy's savior. He will protect her from this psychotic villain. Jeffrey does prove instrumental in cracking the mystery of the severed ear, which ultimately liberates Dorothy from Frank.

In the end, Sandy is an angel of light and she rescues Jeffrey from the dark world he is briefly caught in and Dorothy is reunited with her family. It is Sandy's vision that leads them from darkness. She speaks of robins filling the world with light and love. In the final scene, with Sandy and Jeffrey enjoying a benign suburban day, we see a robin. At least, it looks like a robin. Closer inspection reveals, however, this is a mechanical robin. It sits in the window sill, poised for flight with a big, fat, struggling beetle caught in its beak.

In a press release from Paramount Pictures, David Lynch said the script suggested "that within people, strange things that we don't believe can happen, can happen. You know, like there are horrible situations that human beings can get into, but they get out of them too, and I guess that it's part of what *Blue Velvet* is all about."

Perhaps that was what Isabella saw in the role: a way out.

CHAPTER 2

A LIGHT IN THE SHADOWS

Isabella Rossellini got the controversial role because she alone was brave enough to risk it in a field of "name" actresses who were afraid it might damage their images. Her portrayal catapulted her into Hollywood's big time. None of it would have happened, however, if fate hadn't brought Isabella and David together.

It's an old Hollywood cliche—success is due to a lot of luck and being in the right place at the right time. When Isabella first laid eyes on David Lynch, she had no idea who he was. And he did not know who she was.

They were introduced by mutual friends at a restaurant in New York City. David took one look at Isabella and, as he later told Nan Robertson in an October 11, 1986 *New York Times* article, said, "You could be Ingrid Bergman's daughter."

"You idiot!" a friend interjected. "She *is* Ingrid Bergman's daughter."

Not only was Lynch ignorant of Isabella's parentage, he did not know that she was an actress. He thought she was a dancer, because she had said she was in *White Nights* with ballet star Mikhail Baryshnikov and the dancer Gregory Hines, and the film hadn't been released yet.

"Then a week later I saw her picture in *Screen World*," Lynch recalled. I said, "Holy jumpin' George—she's an actress!" Lynch immediately sent her a script, according to an interview with Lynch in an October 1986 issue of *Details*.

Dorothy Vallens was not an easy role for Lynch to cast.

"Before I ever met Isabella," David recalled for Lizzie Borden in a September 23, 1986 article in *The Village Voice*, "I interviewed a lot of women for the part. Then I discovered that the person had to be foreign so she would be more lost and more vulnerable. It would be easier for her to slip into something dark because she was on unsure footing in a dark country. Also, she would have a mystery being foreign and that is really magical."

Lynch found it hard to convince established actresses to consider the emotionally charged role. Whoever played Dorothy had to be willing to delve deep inside to bare a dark side that is rarely explored in films.

"A lot of them were intrigued by the role and drawn to it, but were apprehensive about being Dorothy for as long as it would take to make the film," Lynch told Jacob Paul in "Rossellini: Intrepid Italian," an article that appeared in *Movietime Magazine* in September 1986.

Isabella had no fear, only excitement about playing a role as challenging as Dorothy Vallens. She loved the script at first sight.

Just as Ingrid Bergman knew she had to work with Roberto Rossellini more than three decades earlier, Isabella knew she had to work with David Lynch. Lynch's feelings were mutual.

"With Isabella, something just seemed right about it for her. She had to do it," Lynch said.

Lynch—to his eternal delight—found that all the actors he ultimately cast in *Blue Velvet* loved the script right off the bat, no small compliment in a town where hundreds of scripts line the office walls of Hollywood's top-echelon movie moguls. Even Bobby Vinton wanted to be in the film. He wanted to play the role of Frank.

There is one particularly powerful moment in the film when Isabella—naked and bruised from a beating—was required to walk across Jeffrey's lawn. She is exposed from head to toe, not only physically, but emotionally, as well. The scene in the film owes its inspiration to the memory of an event that Lynch has kept in mind since his childhood.

"When I was little, I think it was in Boise, Idaho, I was with my younger brother, and we saw a woman walking naked on the street," Lynch said. "My brother started crying. That was Dorothy, right there. It was so strange, but it was also strange my brother started crying. She was crazed, something bad had happened . . . we both knew that she didn't even know who she was or that she was naked. The same as Dorothy."

Critics and moviegoers have come back to the scene again and again. Feminists declare the scene exploitative, whereas Janet Maslin at *The New York Times* found the film filled with "deadpan humor" and "brilliance." One director even demanded of Lynch: "Why didn't you light her better?" "One of the sickest things to me," Lynch told Jack Mathews of *The Los Angeles Times* in a September 26, 1986 article, "is when people say, 'How can you show her naked like this, she looks so bad, she's not a Playboy bunny' . . . The same people turn around and say, 'Why aren't there more realistic things in movies?' I want to show a lot of things in films, not just plastic Hollywood things. Women feel so good about Isabella doing that. I think they say, 'Thank God somebody had the guts to go and do something that isn't plastic.'"

Isabella is, without question, an actress with courage. It was the making of *Blue Velvet* that tested—and strengthened—this courage.

"When I came out of the bushes totally naked, I felt like a slab of beef hanging," the actress told David Hutchings in an October 1986 *People* magazine article. "There was nothing sexy about it. It would have felt like a sin if he was going to do a nude scene to titilate the public. . . . It was very important for me to come out with a gesture of total helplessness."

While Isabella was determined to take the part, her agent was aghast when his client first mentioned the role of Dorothy. But, like her father, Isabella has always been fascinated by the deep and sometimes raging emotions trapped just below the surface in the world of human relationships. Like her mother, Isabella had strong ideas about what was best for her as far as her career was concerned. That being the case, she fired her agent and hired a new one.

"There is this idea that you have to play heroines or women who succeed, but I felt a tremendous compassion for this character who is nothing like me," Isabella said.

It was precisely that fact—that Dorothy was not Isa-bella—that allowed the actress to play the role. "It would be difficult to be beaten up, difficult to take your clothes off, difficult to be Isabella doing these things."

Janet Maslin, film critic for the *New York Times*, wrote in a review that appeared on September 17, 1986, "Mr. Hopper and Ms. Rossellini are so far outside the bounds of ordinary acting here that their performances are best understood in terms of sheer lack of inhibition; both give themselves entirely over to the material, which seems to be exactly what's called for."

It was David's vision as an artist that attracted Isabella in the first place. It was also that vision that inspired and enabled her to "totally inhabit" the role of Dorothy.

Isabella understood the director's vision from their first meeting. Yet his is not a vision, or a mind, that is easy to explain, or easy to pin down.

"When David shows you something, it looks very weird, but we all seem to relate to it," Isabella told Stephen Schiff in "The Weird Dreams of David Lynch," a March 1987 article that appeared in *Vanity Fair*. "The brain flashes things in your mind that are so violent," she said. "I don't know how many times I've seen my funeral, or murder. Your mind attracts these strange things—actually, you enjoy them—but you usually just dismiss them and say they're ridiculous. David seems to be able to capture them.

"With David you understand without really understanding him. Most of the time, you see a film and you ask lots of questions, then you talk to intelligent friends and you think, you read, and then you have it all figured out. Not with David. He just reaches that spot where there is no answer."

Blue Velvet was filmed in Lumberton, North Carolina, a

real town with real people. Perhaps it was during the shoot—when Isabella's days were spent working hard to create a new celluloid reality—that she began falling in love with the man, not the director.

It is impossible to pinpoint the precise second when feelings deepen and love becomes a possibility, not just a remote fantasy. For Isabella and David, perhaps that second happened the night they filmed the infamous scene.

Hundreds of people came to watch. The hot sun had set and the night was cooling off. A refreshing wind blew from the Gulf Stream. Some people had even packed a picnic. They sat in plastic fold-up chairs behind the rope cordoning off the area where the camera would dolly back and forth on a miniature railroad track.

Everyone was polite. Southern hospitality was a principle the folks of Lumberton lived by. Besides, it wasn't every day that a Hollywood movie crew came to Lumberton. And certainly all the extra jobs and revenue were welcomed with open arms. Naturally, the residents would have preferred seeing Robert Redford or Paul Newman grace their streets, but these "new kids"—Isabella Rossellini and Kyle MacLachlan—were "just fine."

Kids played tag while the grown-ups waited for the assistant director to yell "Quiet on the set." The residents were already old pros at this movie lingo. They knew that when the camera operator said, "We've got speed," that meant the film was rolling in the camera. "Action" was soon to follow.

That night was different.

One of the stars, the one the old-timers recall looking so much like Ingrid Bergman, actually crossed that dividing line and came into their midst. One by one, she told the townspeople of Lumberton they might not want to stick around for the next scene, explaining it might be offensive to them. She knew the conservative Southern Baptists lining the streets three deep would not want their children to see her stumbling around, naked and bruised. They looked at her politely, not quite comprehending what it was she wanted them to do. Did she want them to leave? They had brought their kids. Kids don't like to be disappointed. They had packed cold chicken and potato salad to munch on between takes. This was a rare event and the townfolks had gathered to watch it just as they gathered every year to watch the Fourth of July fireworks. With all due respect, their eyes said, they would stay and watch.

Isabella had no choice but to give up her small crusade. She had to prepare herself emotionally for the very scene she was warning them against.

When the director yelled "Action," the townspeople were stunned by the scene unfolding before them. Isabella stumbled across the lawn toward Jeffrey. Her mind in a fog and her body looking badly beaten, she walked like a woman whose spirit has been broken.

"These people had brought their children and grandparents," Isabella recalled. "After the third take, they were all gone."

It had been David Lynch, the visionary, who led her through the treacherous emotional waters of *Blue Velvet*—who applauded her daring, her courage, and her vulnerability when the scene was shot. Perhaps that was when their love was born. Two artists looking at each other, each inspired by the struggle of the other to create something from nothing and tell a story with meaning.

Just as Ingrid Bergman never lost faith in Roberto

Rossellini's vision—despite his professional annihilation by the critics—the same was true for Isabella. She never lost faith in Lynch's vision.

"It relates to a strange side of the emotions, but it is very touching," she said.

Lynch challenged Isabella as an actress, but he also saw facets of her that no one else had ever seen.

"He took my beauty and discovered something comical in it," Isabella said. "And also something a bit repellant. That fascinated me. I like to extend myself as an actress and David really helped me. He is the director who takes me the furthest. With him, you feel lit up right away. You sense you are with someone original."

It is no wonder Isabella fell in love with David Lynch. Neither is it any wonder David Lynch fell in love with Isabella—an actress with a rare courage to explore a role so dark most actresses ran from it. That the two of them should become lovers seemed natural.

David Lynch could well be the American counterpart to Isabella's father, Roberto Rossellini. In fact, before his death in 1977, Roberto gave Lynch a scholarship to study in Rome after seeing *The Elephant Man*, the first film Lynch was hired to direct.

Like Rossellini, this young director created a film classic at the beginning of his career. His first film, *Eraserhead*, is still shown in theaters all over the world. Roberto Rossellini was artistically ignored for many years, but, today, no one denies the awesome power and beauty of the trilogy he made after World War II: *Open City*, *Paisan*, and *Germany Year Zero*. His technique, which combined storytelling with a documentary approach, marked the beginning of a new way of making films. Film students consider him the father of neorealism. Many of the principles of filmmaking he introduced with his trilogy are taken for granted today.

Like Roberto Rossellini, Lynch is inspired by the Mr. Hyde side of human nature and seeks to expose the textures, conflicts, and contradictions in relationships, shunning anything that is starkly black-and-white. Lynch doesn't believe that issues are ever black-and-white.

Lynch is a warm, engaging man, as was Isabella's father. His brilliance does not isolate him. While both explored the dark side of the human psyche in their films, it is light and joy that mark their relationships in real life.

The actress speaks only of the light matters concerning them. She learned from her mother many years ago not to speak to the press of matters too close to the heart unless you want the whole world to know about it. Making an exception, Isabella spoke with the writer Stephen Schiff about her relationship with Lynch. David and she even posed together for pictures.

"He's very careful about the way his collar stands and it has to be white, and it has to be a special kind of white shirt," Isabella told Schiff. "He is not weird at all as a person. A lot of people ask me. He's such a serene, calm, very sweet man. I know he must be thinking about the dark side of things, but I have never found his dark side. Never."

Critics, however, have charged that David exploited their personal relationship in *Blue Velvet*, something Isabella has vehemently denied. "It is not true that David Lynch wanted to humiliate me. I never felt exploited or abused."

To Isabella, Lynch was not her exploiter, but her savior. Lynch's powerful vision and his humanity as a person enabled Isabella to discover a dormant part of herself: her passion for acting. It's a passion that is palpable in every color-drenched frame of *Blue Velvet*.

"My problem with the acting is that I felt for a very long time I didn't have a passion," Isabella explained. "That was because I was intimidated by my mother's big talent and then my father didn't want me to be an actress. I don't know for what reason. I think it was jealousy . . . But what was also hard for me was the attention. A film student can make his own film, he can make as many mistakes as he wants—but he doesn't have the press covering it. If I do something on film I get more attention than a beginning actress because of my mother and all that."

By casting her as Dorothy in *Blue Velvet*, David gave Isabella Rossellini more than just a role in a movie. The role of Dorothy acted as a beacon of light for Isabella. The closer she moved toward the light—embracing her own passions—the farther she moved from the shadows of her parents' love—where she had been standing all her life.

CHAPTER 3

INGRID

I ngrid Bergman loved to daydream as a child. She lived in a world of make believe, where she was always queen. It was Ingrid's way of conquering loneliness, for she learned solitude at a young age. To cope, she escaped into fantasy, creating the vibrant, laughing friends she lacked in real life.

"As a little girl, I was always being something else," Ingrid recalled years later in *My Story*, her autobiography written with Alan Burgess.

"A bird, or a lamppost, a policeman, a postman, a flowerpot . . . I remember the day I decided to be a small dog. Of course, it all came out of being a lonely child."

It wasn't always that way. Ingrid spent her first three years happily ensconced at Number 3 Strandvägen, in a spacious, sixth-floor apartment above her father's photography studio in Stockholm. Justus and Friedel, her parents, loved each other dearly, in part because their marriage was achieved only after much sorrow.

Friedel fell in love with Justus when she found him painting in the woods. Friedel was exploring the outskirts of Stockholm while on vacation from her home in Hamburg. She peered through the trees at this unusual man painting feverishly amidst the shadows. She was captivated.

Returning to her home in Germany, Friedel learned that her parents viewed Justus as a poor Bohemian artist with few prospects. To win Friedel's hand, Justus had to prove himself capable of taking care of a wife, and give up his dream of being an artist. For the next seven years, he struggled to open a successful photography business at Number 3 Strandvägen. Surprisingly, he proved to be a good businessman and eventually Friedel's parents deemed him good enough for their daughter.

By the time Ingrid entered the world on August 29, 1913 Justus and Friedel were nearly overcome with joy. All new parents are mesmerized by their creations, but Justus and Friedel were truly enthralled. Just as they had had to wait to become man and wife, they had to wait for a healthy baby. Friedel lost her first two children, one at birth and one a week after birth. After seven years of marriage, Friedel finally gave birth to a healthy baby girl.

Ingrid was an exuberant child. By the age of three, her energy was barely containable. She loved to talk. When her father sang to her, she would hum along and clap her hands. The singing stopped when her mother died.

Friedel Adler Bergman died when Ingrid was three of a liver ailment that puzzled doctors at the time. Justus used one of the first movie cameras commonly available to the public to shoot footage of Ingrid as she said good-bye to her mother. As if foreshadowing the quiet loneliness of the years to come, Ingrid, a tiny figure dressed in a dark mourning dress, walked to her mother's grave and laid white flowers across the freshly turned sod. She stood in the shadow of her mother's carved tombstone, not quite sure what was happening. That tiny figure had no way of knowing she was to grow up in the long shadow of a love she lost early on. She could only remember, deep in her heart, the simplicity and warmth of her mother's love, an all-encompassing love she would spend a lifetime seeking.

"She was a sad child and so shy," remembers Disa Lauhren, one of Ingrid's classmates at the prestigious Palm-grenska Samskolan school in Stockholm, who was quoted in Laurence Leamer's *As Time Goes By.* "But when she played, she always played like a star . . . We played, but all the time Ingrid was outside by herself, acting."

It took many years for Justus to see beyond his own pain and heartache. When he did, he realized that Ingrid was much too solemn for a little girl. Seven years after Friedel's death, Justus hired Greta Danielsson, an aspiring actress and singer, as Ingrid's governess. Justus wanted the house to resonate with eighteen-year-old Greta's laughter and high spirits. Greta did her best to draw Ingrid from the fantasy world in which she was so frequently lost, but Ingrid was a remote child. Though she came to love Greta, she could never give up her dream world. It was a momentous day when she discovered her fantasies could be transferred into reality. Ingrid discovered acting.

"My eyes popped out," Ingrid said, recalling in her autobiography, *My Story*, the time Justus took her to the theater. From the minute the curtain went up, Ingrid was spellbound. Justus was not surprised when Ingrid, at the first intermission, turned to him and proudly declared, "Papa. Papa, that's what I'm going to do!"

Ingrid soon learned of the Royal Dramatic, Sweden's most famous theater, which stood at the head of Strandvägen Avenue, as if beckoning to Ingrid from the end of her own street. Ingrid would watch the ebullient actors on their way to their evening performances, preening as they caught sight of themselves in the window of the small photography shop.

Soon after, Ingrid discovered the Roda Kvarn (Red Mill). This movie theater, with its plush seats and thick carpets, was more like a great opera house. She would beg her father to take her to see all the silent films of Charlie Chaplin and Mary Pickford as well as films by the Swedish masters Victor Sjöström and Mauritz Stiller.

Ingrid wrote in her diary as a young girl and recalls in *My Story* that she wrote about the day she would perform on stage and "the public would sit there and see this new Sarah Bernhardt."

Justus encouraged Ingrid's acting ambitions in more ways than he probably knew. In later years, Ingrid came to believe that her father could have been a great painter had he not been forced to give up his artistic dreams in order to win Friedel's hand in marriage. As a result of his own thwarted creativity, Justus lived vicariously through his child. He encouraged her to follow her dreams as he himself had not. This gift would turn out to be Ingrid's real legacy from her father.

"It was my father's enthusiasm over my playacting that turned me into an actress," Ingrid admitted in her autobiography.

Justus stunned everyone except Ingrid when, at the age of fifty-three, he fell in love with Greta, Ingrid's governess. Friedel—who had been dead ten years—would have applauded, but those who carried her memory in their time-frozen minds disapproved.

Greta was just a girl in love. "We fell in love and it was very difficult," Greta told Laurence Leamer. "He was so handsome. We had so much to speak about. I cared for him very much, but I was much younger. He wanted to marry me . . . I said marriage is impossible."

Greta left to pursue a singing career and Ingrid escaped into playacting. She was a princess, she was a savior, she was a beautiful woman with men falling to kiss the ground she walked on. She was most assuredly not a motherless little girl.

When Ingrid was twelve, her father showed her an X-ray plate. It was his. "You see," he said, "This is a cancer growing here. And, darling, pretty soon, I won't be able to get any food down into my stomach. So you see that's serious."

Ingrid didn't understand that her father was telling her he was going to die. She looked at her father and tried to cheer him up. Looking at the X-ray, she pointed out the obvious: "But look," she said, "There's lots of room this way. The food can get in this way, of course it can." Justus couldn't bear to say more to his beloved daughter, as Ingrid recalled in her autobiography.

Like father, like daughter. This trait, a desire to shield loved ones from pain would be adopted by Ingrid. Years later, Ingrid couldn't bear to hurt her first child Pia by telling her she was pregnant by another man. Ingrid did not tell Pia until she had already learned the truth through the media.

As a girl of twelve, Ingrid did not realize how serious her father's condition was until he lay on his deathbed. The end came quickly. As Justus and Friedel's relatives hovered nearby in a deathwatch, Greta and Ingrid sat at Justus's bedside, each holding a hand, occasionally stroking his arm.

"I remember my father turned his head to look at Greta, and then he turned his head to look at me, and I smiled at him," Ingrid said years later in her autobiography. "And that was the end."

Ingrid was a solemn presence at her father's funeral. It did not seem possible she had lost her mother and now her father. Months later, Ingrid lost the woman she had come to call "mama," after her own mother died; her aunt Ellen.

Ellen Bergman, Justus's sister, the only one of thirteen brothers and sisters who never married, moved in with the Bergmans after Friedel died. Ellen spent years looking after Ingrid. One night, six months after Justus's death, Ingrid was awakened by her aunt's cries. Ingrid tried to comfort the woman in her arms as she struggled for breath. It was no use. Her aunt Ellen had suffered a fatal heart attack. By the time Ingrid's uncle arrived, Ellen Bergman had died.

"It was a terrible shock, and I think, inside, I really took a long time to get over it," Ingrid said in her autobiography.

It is no wonder that, years later, Ingrid's friends remember how she loved to laugh, as if laughing could keep back the pain and the loneliness, the *Ensambet*, as it's called in Sweden.

Ingrid moved in with her Uncle Otto and Aunt Hulda and their five children. She grew close to her cousin Britt, who later in life cared for Ingrid during her final days, when she was crippled by cancer.

"In our house, she was just a sister," Britt told Laurence Leamer. "We took it for granted. We were fine together. She was very sensitive as a girl. I had a feeling that she felt very much. She had her fantasy life. She lived in another world."

Ingrid's new life was difficult for her. She had no mother or father. She was living with relatives. Certainly, Ingrid was loved but Otto and Hulda had five children of their own and there was only so much attention that could be given each child.

"She was at a difficult age when she came to her uncles," Greta recalled to Laurence Leamer. "There were so many children. Before she had been the only one."

Ingrid found herself lonely and unhappy. She found solace in the endless riches of her old friends, her imagination.

"The contrast between my acting exhibitions and my normal behavior was so different that it was unbelievable," Ingrid recalled in her autobiography. "I was the shyest human being ever invented. If people asked me what my name was, I'd blush scarlet."

It was Greta who helped Ingrid bridge the gap between the world of amateur playacting and the world of professional filmmaking, in spite of the fact that Uncle Otto wanted Ingrid to be "sensible" and pursue a secretarial job before settling down into a good marriage.

Greta was making a living as a singer as well as an actress. When she landed a small role at Filmindustri (the Swedish Film Industry), she told the director she could bring a friend to help film a scene in which a dozen extras were needed.

When Greta told Ingrid she'd gotten her hired as an extra for the day, Ingrid could barely sleep the night before she was to appear at the studio.

From the moment Ingrid walked onto the set, she was mesmerized. She loved the lights, the cameras, the props, but most of all, she loved the actors, those ethereal creatures who got to spend their days pretending to be other than what they were.

"I must be an actress," Ingrid recalled telling Greta in her autobiography. The fact she was actually paid for her work was almost unfathomable to Ingrid, who had blissfully roamed around the studio all afternoon after her scene was shot.

Knowing she would need help to become an actress, Ingrid wanted rigorous classical training—unlike some of the Hollywood actresses of today who rely only on their beauty. She dreamed of joining the Royal Dramatic School. In 1933, there were seventy-five actors and actresses vying for the eight openings. Ingrid spent hundreds of hours working on her audition. She even hired a private drama teacher as well as a gymnastics coach to help her prepare.

After what seemed like an interminable wait, the big moment was finally at hand. Ingrid stood behind the curtain in the imposing Royal Dramatic School and watched an aspiring actor pour out his heart and soul. A row of twenty judges sat in darkness behind the powerful klieg lights heating up the stage. When her name was announced, Ingrid could barely hear over the pounding of her own heart. She'd imagined this moment a hundred times. Her entire future hinged on it. Either she was chosen or she had to do as her uncle wished.

Ingrid recalled the moment in her autobiography. "I pause and get out my first line, then I take a quick glance down over the footlights at the jury. And I can't believe it. They aren't paying the slightest attention to me . . . I hear the voice of the chairman of the jury: 'Stop it. Stop it. That's enough.'"

Tears welling in her eyes, Ingrid ran from the stage. She ran all the way to the nearby harbor. Having failed her audition, she was desperate. She stared down at the water.

"And I knew there's only one thing to do," Ingrid recalled. "Throw myself into the water and commit suicide."

Ingrid steeled herself for the shock of the cold water. She stared at the rippling waves. Then she realized the water was dirty. That wouldn't do at all. She wasn't about to be pulled from the water, a dirty mess for all the world to see.

Ingrid's desperation didn't last long. When she returned home, she found out she'd made it through the first cut. She would go on to win a spot in the class from the sheer force of her auditions.

Ingrid adored drama school. It was the family she never had. As she once described it: "I felt I belonged to something at last." Much as she loved being part of her new family, however, Ingrid did not complete her studies; professional offers started coming in almost from the beginning. And then she fell in love.

It was not love at first sight. Sitting with her cousin and two friends at the Grand Hotel in Stockholm, Ingrid smiled shyly at Petter Lindstrom, all six-foot-two of him. They danced. Petter was a wonderful dancer. Years later, he would be known as the one to dance with at star-studded Hollywood parties.

On that first date, Ingrid learned her handsome, twenty-six-year-old escort was not only a dentist, he was also an associate professor at the Dental College of the Karolinska Institute in Stockholm, where he was a student of medicine as well. Ingrid found Petter's professional stability very appealing. She knew that Uncle Otto and Aunt Hulda would approve. They still thought of her acting as a sin, though they had come to accept her career since she seemed to be making her way already in Sweden.

Ingrid soon began to rely on Petter's advice regarding her career. Together, they were an impressive complement of talents. Petter encouraged Ingrid at every turn and she trusted his experience and judgment. At some point, this trust blossomed into love. They began a three-year courtship that included the traditional one-year engagement. They walked down the aisle on July 10, 1937. Ingrid, twenty-one years old when they exchanged their vows, was already somewhat well-known in Sweden, having made six films. The tiny church in Strode, Petter's home town, was packed for their wedding.

Five months into their marriage, Ingrid became pregnant. She gave birth to a healthy baby girl on September 20, 1938. The baby was christened Friedel Pia. Before the baby was born, however, Ingrid was already being courted by the Hollywood establishment, a courtship she found difficult to resist. David O. Selznick, the famous producer, called on Ingrid some time after *Intermezzo* was released. It was Ingrid's sixth Swedish film. Even though Ingrid was nearly nine months pregnant, the indefatigable Selznick was trying to lure her to Hollywood. Thus began a relationship that would launch Ingrid Bergman's international career.

Kay Brown acted as Selznick's liaison to Ingrid. Before Ingrid traveled to America, touted as Selznick's bright new star, Kay had qualms about her role in wooing Ingrid to Hollywood.

"You know, you've got a lovely home and a lovely baby," Kay told Ingrid. "You're happy here. If I were you, I would think it over very carefully."

Looking back years later, Kay recalled to Alan Burgess for Ingrid's autobiography, "You can't conceive that child-like air of innocence which surrounded Ingrid."

Ingrid, however, knew what she wanted. "Well if there are people as nice as you in America and in Hollywood, then I'm sure I shall like it, so I shall go and take the risk."

David Selznick's newest import sailed to New York

aboard the *Queen Mary*, leaving her new husband and six-month-old baby behind. Her life would never be the same.

Ingrid was introduced to American audiences in 1939. She again played the role that first caught Selznick's attention in an American remake of *Intermezzo*, this time with Leslie Howard as her co-star. She was to become a star adored and cherished by the American public over the next ten years as she made fourteen pictures, the most famous of which is *Casablanca*.

After she made *Joan of Arc*, a seventy-five-foot-high image of Ingrid as Joan was erected above Times Square. To Americans, Ingrid was a symbol of goodness, the woman she had played so many times. She was vulnerable, alone, a woman who could be lured into adulterous affairs yet still retain her moral strength and emerge emotionally victorious, her image unscarred.

It was inconceivable that Ingrid could ever disappoint her public, that they could ever abandon her. Inconceivable, but not impossible. Ingrid did more than disappoint her public. She appalled them. And they did more than abandon her. They vilified her with all the wrath of a jilted lover.

CHAPTER
4

INGRID IN EXILE

I ngrid listened to the low drone of the prop engines as the TWA plane left the runway. How many times had she boarded an airplane, always leaving behind her husband, Petter, and their daughter, Pia? The jet soared above Los Angeles before banking east for New York, final destination Rome. They were familiar to Ingrid, these grand comings and goings, yet this time, it was different. She was off to start a new career, of sorts, leaving the big bankrolls of Hollywood for the world of low-budget art films. And she was leaving an old love for a new love, one with whom she would create three children. One child from that marriage would follow in her footsteps. Her name would be Isabella. Staring out the window, Ingrid could not see what her new life would bring. She thought only of all the starts *and stops she had already lived through. This seemed like just one more. But it wasn't. Nothing would ever be the same.*

The lights of Los Angeles grew smaller and smaller with each added mile she put between herself and her old life. Ingrid thought of Roberto as she peered out the window. She sat, her hands folded, her expression calm. No one would suspect that only hours earlier, Ingrid had walked out on her twelve-year marriage. She had taken most of her clothes, furs, jewelry, and all her scrapbooks. And yet, neither Petter nor Ingrid truly realized that nothing would ever be the same for them.

The romance of Roberto Rossellini and Ingrid Bergman had begun before they ever met. It began, even if Ingrid didn't know it, with her husband at her side, as she sat watching *Open City* in the spring of 1948. Ingrid was a star, but she was bored. She had made numerous big-budget, star-studded Hollywood films. It wasn't enough. She wanted more.

"I would've died to try something new," she recalled in *My Story.*

Roberto Rossellini, the visionary of neorealism, unknowingly fit the bill.

"The realism and simplicity of *Open City* was heart shocking," Ingrid recalled in her autobiography. "There was darkness and shadows. Sometimes you couldn't hear. Sometimes you couldn't even see it. But that's the way it is in life . . . you can't always see and hear, but you know that something almost beyond understanding is going on. . . . It was as if you were there, involved in what was going on, and you wept and bled for them. . . ."

Ingrid wanted to work with Roberto Rossellini, so she did what any major, bankable Hollywood star would do.

She wrote him a letter saying, "If you need a Swedish actress who speaks English very well, who has not forgotten her German, who is not very understandable in French, and who, in Italian knows only *ti amo*, I am ready to come and make a film with you," Ingrid said in her autobiography.

Ingrid's letter traveled a strange journey before finding its way to Roberto. Ingrid sent her letter to Minerva Films. "The night my letter arrived Minerva Films burnt down," Ingrid recalled in her autobiography. "Big blaze. Nothing but ashes." As workmen cleared away the charred debris, however, Ingrid's letter was found, a bit blackened around the edges but intact. Roberto's response was short and swift. The cable arrived at Ingrid's home at 1220 Benedict Canyon Drive in Beverly Hills, on May 8, 1948. It read: "It is absolutely true that I dreamed to make a film with you. . . ."

Ingrid arrived at Ciampino Airport outside Rome in March of 1949. Roberto, as well as hundreds of effusive Italians, greeted her. To the exceedingly religious Italians, Ingrid Bergman was practically an American saint, if not Joan of Arc, or the saintly, devoted nun, Sister Benedict, she had portrayed in *The Bells of St. Mary's*.

While Roberto drove his sports car through back streets, he reeled off one story after another about the colorful history of Rome and its ancient glories. He beguiled her with magical tales of the early days of the Roman Empire, the city of the gods.

Without a doubt, he was charming, but as even his sister Marcella told Laurence Leamer in his book *As Time Goes By*, "People would say he's charming like a snake with little birds." Roberto was known as a ladies' man. Ingrid

Bergman, however, was the first woman who fell prey to his charms who was a bigger name than he was.

As it turned out, she always would be.

Roberto and Ingrid started filming *Stromboli*, their first film together, in early April 1949. By April 13, the gossip columnists reported a romance rumored to have sprung up between Ingrid and Roberto. It was the first time Ingrid Bergman had ever been the subject of negative publicity. While Ingrid and Roberto made a film with no script and a sparse story at a remote location on the edge of a real volcano, Petter tried to call his wife. Both he and the world wondered what was happening. There were no telephones on the island. The gossip spread like wildfire. A "saint" behaving like a sinner, a fallen woman, is big news. The paparazzi were merciless.

Kay Brown, David Selznick's original liaison to Ingrid, traveled to Stromboli in an attempt to talk some sense into Ingrid, whom she had wooed from Sweden to Hollywood over a decade earlier.

"Our conversations were so useless," Kay recalled to Alan Burgess. "I would say 'Ingrid, this is ridiculous. You'll lose your husband and your daughter and your career and everything,' and Ingrid would simply reply, 'Yes, I know.' To me, she looked so lost and wan and bewildered."

Ingrid imagined that life with Roberto would be all magic and passion. Roberto was just as obsessed with filmmaking and storytelling as she was. They saw life in the same light. They were soulmates. Film, to them, was the light. Ingrid thought her passion was all-consuming and neverending. She was mistaken. Within a few weeks, her romantic visions crumbled as the press strung her up and left her out to dry. Her fall from grace was swift and brutal.

All hope of avoiding a scandal ended in June, when Ingrid became pregnant, just two months into the shooting of *Stromboli*. Her first son, Robertino, was born on February 2, 1950. Her divorce from Petter had still not come through, thus Robertino was considered illegitimate.

On March 14, 1950, Senator Edwin C. Johnson of Colorado used the Senate floor to denounce Ingrid Bergman. Echoing the thoughts of a nation, he said, as Laurence Leamer noted in Ingrid's biography. "It was upsetting to have our most popular, but pregnant movie queen, her condition the result of an illicit affair, play the part of a cheap, chiseling female . . ."

Senator Johnson referred to the "vile and unspeakable Rossellini who sets an all-time low in shameless exploitation and disregard for good public morals. . . ." Furthermore, the Senator called Ingrid "one of the most powerful women on earth today—I regret to say, a powerful influence for evil." Senator Johnson was voicing an outrage not uncommon among her fans, many of whom felt betrayed by her indiscretion set against the backdrop of the sexually conservative 1950s.

Petter still tried to get his wife back. At first, he refused to consent to a divorce. Ingrid finally wrote him telling him that their marriage was over. That should have been obvious to him, considering the imminent divorce proceedings, but Ingrid had never told Petter in her own words that she no longer wished to be married to him.

"I wanted Petter to know that I was leaving him, that I was unfaithful," Ingrid recalled. "So I wrote that letter telling him the truth, and a little later a second one that said,

'I have found the place where I want to live, these people are my people, and I want to stay here and I'm sorry. . . .'

"There were so many years when I was just waiting to find somebody who would make me leave. Roberto did that. I didn't think it would upset the whole world."

The world saw photos of a serene and beautiful Ingrid splashed across the pages of *Life* magazine. The truth was not nearly so pretty. Ingrid was being torn apart.

"It was absolute hell," she recalled in her autobiography. "I cried so much I thought there couldn't be any tears left. I felt the newspapers were right. I'd abandoned my husband and child. I was an awful woman . . . but I hadn't meant it that way.

"People thought I was having such a marvelous time being in love when all I did was cry because the real guilt of the offense was grinding me down. I felt terrible about all the people who wrote me. I'd ruined their movie [*Stromboli*]. I'd ruined myself; my career was finished forever . . . . here I was stuck and didn't know what to do about it."

Ingrid cried for months. She was thirty-six years old, at the height of her power as a woman and as an actress, yet her life was a shambles, a tragic contrast to Isabella at the same age—a newly discovered "hot property." •

Ingrid's twelve-year marriage to Dr. Petter Aron Lindstrom ended and Pia publicly rejected her, telling all the world, during a custody hearing: "I don't love my mother. . . . I like her. . . . I haven't seen her enough to really love her."

When Pia renounced her, Ingrid was heartbroken. She spent a great deal of time staring out the window of her small apartment, where she was virtually a prisoner. If she so much as set a toe outside the door, hordes of photographers would descend on her like vultures.

She attempted to console herself with the anticipation of the release of *Stromboli*. She prayed that her fans would stand by her, but there was to be no respite. Roberto and Ingrid's labor of love, *Stromboli*, opened February 15, 1950, in three hundred theaters, just thirteen days after their "love child" was born. Not surprisingly, the film was panned by critics and rejected by Ingrid's once-loyal public.

On February 16, 1950, a *New York Times* film critic called *Stromboli* "incredibly feeble, inarticulate, uninspiring and painfully banal." The film was a bomb. Years later, Rossellini would be hailed as a genius and acknowledged for his work—including *Stromboli*. But that was many years away.

Faced with scathing, vicious reviews, Ingrid did the only thing she could. She worked at her marriage. She tried to ignore her shattered career and the pain she had inflicted on others through her actions. Faced with the loss of acting, she buried herself in distractions, as she had done since she was a young girl and lost both parents. She had always loved losing herself within the confines of another identity. Yet even that escape was to be denied the fallen angel.

Ingrid did not make a Hollywood film for seven years. She had been desperate to play a role that was shocking and new, but her need for artistic growth turned into an international scandal of a magnitude hard to fathom in today's world. She did not realize just how devoted her public was, how shattered they would be by what they perceived as her betrayal and desertion.

Ingrid did work with Roberto, but though she loved his

early work, she had a difficult time working without scripts and making movies on shoestring budgets. To make matters worse, everything they attempted ended in resounding failure. None of the films they made together dealt with the kind of material Ingrid had grown accustomed to in Hollywood. And none of them lived up to the brilliance Rossellini had wrought with his war trilogy: *Open City*, *Paisan*, and *Germany Year Zero*.

Their artistic collaborations floundered, as did their marriage, though it took Ingrid and Roberto several years to admit it. Ingrid did not like facing painful truths. Fiorella Mariani, the daughter of Roberto's sister, Marcella, remembers how Ingrid was during this time.

"You could never see what she really felt," Fiorella told Laurence Leamer. "She could be bursting with laughter and holding a tragedy within. She was afraid of suffering. She was afraid of evil. She couldn't stand discussion of it. She was afraid of violence, of things that maybe she couldn't say."

Ingrid hated unpleasantness. When faced with it, she became almost paralyzed, which explains why she could not face Petter when she ran off to meet her lover in Rome, why she could not say good-bye to Pia, a daughter she dearly loved, and why she could not extricate herself from a scandal that rocked a nation. She had had enough pain as a child. She couldn't willingly face more of it.

"I don't think I've ever seen a woman as ravaged with feelings of guilt, love and remorse," Greg Bautzer, Ingrid's attorney recalled to Alan Burgess. "But who knows what happens to a woman hopelessly in love? Rossellini was a Svengali. She was like a prisoner."

The exiled star was pregnant again by 1952. Since her

estrangement from Pia, she desperately wanted to have another little girl. When Ingrid grew unusually rotund, the doctor realized she was carrying twins. It was a difficult pregnancy and labor was finally induced on June 18, 1952.

Ingrid gave birth to two strapping, healthy baby girls. Isabella Fiorella Elettra Giovanna weighed in at seven pounds, three ounces; Isotta Ingrid Frieda Giuliana weighed in at eight pounds, five ounces.

Even at birth, the twins exhibited different natures. Isotta, always called Ingrid, was quiet and calm. She ultimately chose a career in the academic world. Isabella entered the world with a scream that demanded to be heard. A foreshadowing of the future, some might say.

CHAPTER

5

LIKE FATHER, LIKE DAUGHTER

I t is natural to assume that Isabella Rossellini is her mother's daughter. She looks like her mother. She sounds like her mother. And, like her mother, Isabella is an actress. On film, there are moments when, watching Isabella, one sees Ingrid's face, her voice, and her movements. Their cinematic similarities are stunning. When Ingrid was still alive, they resembled each other in small ways—both liked wearing baggy, comfortable clothes—and big ways—they both made Hollywood sit up and take notice. But there are many differences.

Even her looks are mercurial—and misleading. One minute she looks like her mother, the ultimate Swedish beauty, with her luminous eyes, large soft lips, the same wide smile. A second later, however, the chameleon has changed and the spirit of her father is overpowering.

Isabella would be the first to admit she is, perhaps, more her father's daughter. "He is very present with me in terms of the direction he thought my life should go," she told Laurie Winer in "Isabella Rossellini Assesses the Role that Haunted Her," a November 1986 *New York Times* article. "Morally, he's a very strong figure for me. He had incredible understanding and tenderness which I haven't found in any other person."

Roberto Rossellini was an iconoclastic rebel. He knew early in life that he wanted to make films—but only films that captured reality. Filmgoers take that notion for granted today, but in the late thirties and early forties, when Rossellini was learning his craft, realism was the exception and not the norm. The man who was to be dubbed "the father of neorealism" spent his entire career trying to unravel the mystery of human relationships by portraying them as realistically as he possibly could on film.

Roberto Rossellini was, in person, unassuming and bookish. When he wooed and won Ingrid, he was balding and had a small paunch. Countering this appearance was his zeal for life and his love of film. Italians knew him as a passionate, erudite storyteller before the world knew him as a brilliant young director.

Like her father, Isabella is captivated and inspired by the same passions and concerns. Like her father, she loves to take risks. She risked stalling her career before it even got started when she teamed up with David Lynch to make *Blue Velvet*. Not only did she win the role of Dorothy Vallens, but her courageous portrayal of Dorothy made her a star.

Roberto did not live to see how much his daughter emulated his philosophy of life. "You must take calculated risks in life," Roberto Rossellini said in a *New York Times* interview in 1971. "You accept the risk, you accept your fate. Otherwise you will end up doing what other people say to do. You must invest your life for today and for tomorrow. It is a choice one must make."

Roberto Rossellini loved living on the edge, both personally and professionally. He took a risk when he fell in love with Ingrid Bergman. With *Open City*, the young director had just burst upon the international scene as a critically acclaimed filmmaker. Once he and Ingrid joined forces, both personally and professionally, Roberto's later accomplishments were constantly overlooked.

Once hailed as a major talent, one of the best and brightest European directors, Rossellini went into a long career decline during his years with Ingrid Bergman. Believing he was the instrument of Ingrid's demise, the public could not forgive him. It wasn't until after their marriage was annulled that the accolades came and Roberto was finally recognized as a pioneering filmmaker. Roberto made a total of twenty-eight films. Equally important, he was a mentor to such directors as François Truffaut, Michaelangelo Antonioni, and Federico Fellini.

Italian to the core, Roberto Rossellini was gregarious. He loved to talk. He loved to feast. He loved heated political arguments. He loved women. And he loved complaining when he was upset or depressed. He would frequently take to his bed with strange ailments whenever life's struggles wore him down. The son of a respected and affluent architect and builder, he was born in Rome on May 8, 1906.

Roberto broke into the world of filmmaking as a sound-effects technician after serving as an apprentice. He eventually became a technical advisor and made several short films on his own.

At thirty-nine, an age at which many men have settled for less, Roberto finally made his debut as a writer-director with *Open City*, his first major film. He filmed this war classic while Italy was still occupied by Nazis, frequently hiding his camera from the Nazi patrols that stalked the city at night. Rossellini made the film on a shoestring; the total cost was nineteen thousand dollars. When the film was released, Rossellini was called a genius and his star, Anna Magnani, was catapulted to international stardom.

It is no wonder that Ingrid Bergman was awed and stunned when she saw Rossellini's first major feature debut. Sitting in a darkened theater next to Petter, Ingrid watched, awestruck. The film evoked emotions she had tried to forget since childhood, feelings of separation, abandonment, betrayal, and alienation.

Open City revolves around the interwoven lives of three young women during World War II. Pina, played by Anna Magnani, lives a working-class existence. Maria is an out-of-work actress and a drug addict. She is also the kept woman of Manfredi, a Communist who is devoted to the Resistance movement. Lauretta is Maria's friend.

Chaos reigns in their world, which is defined by dislocation and disparity. Theirs is a world where children must tragically grow up before their time. It was perhaps this element that drew Ingrid Bergman so powerfully to Roberto Rossellini. She had been forced to grow up early after losing both her parents at such a young age.

No one escapes the ravages of war in *Open City*. No one hides from the aftershocks. Lives are disrupted and many never recover the balance they had before the bombs came. When Pina falls in love, her marriage plans are thwarted when the Germans mistakenly arrest her fiancé. When Pina runs after the truck carrying her fiancé away, she is shot and killed.

Endless contradictions underscore the film. In one scene, we see a peaceful tableau of family life; in the next, German troops brutally enter and forever shatter that family life as they search out the enemy. Roberto's style is largely devoid of the kind of cinematic effects movie audiences take for granted today. He gave no emphasis to special moments. He didn't believe in it. Consequently, all his scenes are shot with the same level of intensity.

In a 1954 interview in *Cahiers du Cinema*, Roberto said, "I always try to remain impassive; it seemed to me that what is so astonishing, so extraordinary, so moving in human realities is precisely the fact that noble acts and momentous events happen in the same way and produce the same impression as the ordinary facets of everyday life. I then attempt to convey both in the same manner—a method with its very own source of dramatic interest."

Key to Rossellini's vision of filmmaking was the notion that the director should record reality truthfully. "I'm only interested in knowledge," he declared, "but I don't want to interfere with it."

Despite the emotional trauma suffered by the characters in *Open City*, the story ends with unmistakable optimism. The hope lies with the children who live courageously on, even after witnessing such horrors as the execution of a priest involved in the Resistance.

When Ingrid watched *Open City*, it was one of the most emotional experiences of her career. "If there is such a man who can put this on the screen, he must be an absolutely heavenly human being," Ingrid declared in her autobiography.

Still, no one had ever heard of Roberto Rossellini in Hollywood. Ingrid figured he was a one-shot director, perhaps even a fluke.

Ingrid found herself in New York a few months after seeing *Open City*. While taking a break from a radio taping, she stumbled across a small movie theater on Broadway. Reading the credits of a film titled *Paisan*, Ingrid came across Rossellini's name again. As she later told Alan Burgess, "I went in alone, and I sat there once more riveted to my seat."

The second film of Roberto's war trilogy is divided into six episodes, each dealing with aspects of the Allied invasion and liberation of Italy, and each played out in different Italian cities and villages. The first episode, in Sicily, concerns a young Sicilian girl and an American soldier who become lovers, though they do not speak each other's language. He is killed in an instant by a German soldier who sees him light a cigarette. The young girl hides and later shoots a German. The Americans believe the young girl killed their dead friend. In the end, however, the Germans kill the girl and throw her over a cliff into a ravine. The five other episodes that compose the movie are equally bleak.

It is easy to see the similarities in Rossellini's interests as a filmmaker and Isabella's choices as an actress. Isabella is drawn to the same realistic stories of human drama that so captivated her father. And, like her father, Isabella has shouldered a lot of criticism for her choices.

After Roberto's brilliant launch with *Open City*, he gave the public *Paisan*. The critics were quick to accuse him of pessimism, because a sense of hope was absent from *Open City*. Rossellini had no patience with the notion that he was a pessimist.

"I am not a pessimist," he told Vincent Canby. "To perceive evil where it exists is, in my opinion, a form of optimism. I have been criticized for not offering any solution but if I were capable of finding a solution, I wouldn't have made films. I'd have done something else."

Isabella suffered similar criticism after the release of *Blue Velvet*. One could imagine Isabella, and David Lynch for that matter, saying the same words Roberto employed to defend his artistic choices.

Like her father, Isabella is fiercely independent and outspoken. Roberto, no doubt, balanced some of Ingrid's influences on Isabella. Ingrid, by her own admission, was more deferring, more placating.

"Men make women helpless by deciding and telling them what to do," Ingrid recalled in her autobiography. "Men in my life taught me to be independent."

Isabella is more like her father.

"I think I'm very Latin," Isabella told Lawrence Eisenberg in a February 1983 *Cosmopolitan* article entitled "Bella Bella Isabella." "I like people. I laugh a lot. I'm loud and very social. I think I got all that from my father. My mother was very shy and much more reserved and scared. I think pessimistic, too, in a way. I think I'm less frightened, more balanced. She was very vulnerable and I think she didn't hide it."

Like her mother, however, Isabella was stunned by her father's vision when she finally saw his film. Ingrid's feelings simply foreshadowed Isabella's.

Ingrid first saw *Paisan* when she and Petter were planning a second child. They had even picked out a name—Pelle.

And yet she felt drawn to this artist, a man she had never met. When Isabella, as a teenager, saw her father's films, she cried at the power of his artistry.

Once Roberto entered Ingrid's life, it was never the same. When Europe's hottest new director received her letter stating her desire to work with him, he wrote her back immediately and soon after came to visit. He even stayed in Ingrid's guest house. While workmen pounded nails into the future nursery at 1220 Benedict Canyon Drive in Beverly Hills, the themes Roberto explored in his films were still at work on Ingrid's subconscious. She was especially affected by *Paisan*, a film about freedom, both personal and political.

It was the filmmaker who inspired Ingrid to change her life and, as it turned out, risk forever destroying her career. Much later, David Lynch inspired Isabella to take a big risk with the controversial role of Dorothy Vallens. Unlike Ingrid's and Roberto's collaborations, most of Isabella's efforts have been successful.

Years later, Roberto still felt the pain of those early failures. "It was disturbing, of course, but it was also instructive, perhaps—in the long run—even helpful," Roberto Rossellini said. "It forced me to become more rigorous in my work. When you're up against public opinion like that, you either cave in or you do what you have to do and hope that people will come around." It took many years for people to come around but they did—resoundingly. And, like her father, Isabella has worked hard to achieve her dreams, using his example as inspiration.

During the fifties, when Roberto worked almost exclusively with his wife and she with him, his films focused more on the individual. He moved away from the grander themes he explored in *Paisan* and *Open City*—history bearing down on people as history was in the making. In *Stromboli*, as well as the other collaborations with Ingrid, he dealt with forces less tangible than historical events affecting individual lives. He explored issues of personal growth and spirituality.

Roberto was something of a feminist before it was fashionable. The films he made with Ingrid dealt with a solitary woman as she tried to uncover, and forge, her individual identity. The character was always alone, even if she was married. Roberto's sensibilities shaped Isabella. She embraced feminism as a teenager, and as an adult, she has frequently chosen to play independent women facing adversary conditions.

Isabella is convinced that had the "scandal" never happened, her father's films would have been revered earlier. Her favorite film is *Europa, 51*, which her father made with her mother the year before she was born. "Every time I see the movie it makes me cry," she said. "It reminds me of my mother and father and the time they were together."

The great love affair of Isabella's parents was not destined to last, despite the public censure and career setbacks Ingrid and Roberto endured in order to be together. In 1957, while shooting a film in India, Roberto fell in love with Sonali das Gupta, an Indian screenwriter who, as it happened, was married. Another public scandal arose when Sonali became pregnant, leading to the separation and divorce of Ingrid and Roberto in 1958.

Nonetheless, Ingrid stood by Roberto. When the Indian authorities confiscated Roberto's documentary, *India*, it was Ingrid, using all her influence and calling in more than a few favors from friends, who got it back. Ingrid never lost her respect for Roberto Rossellini as a filmmaker.

No longer married to America's Joan of Arc, Roberto

won both critical and popular acclaim in 1959 with *General della Rovere*. With this film, he moved away from the exclusively individual concerns he had explored in film with Ingrid to examine, once again, his characters' relationships to historical events. *General della Rovere* marked a return to the material he had handled so successfully with his World War II trilogy.

Roberto never again strayed from the world of low-budget films. Though he may have felt betrayed by the producers who refused to finance his feature films, he continued to grow as an artist.

"I am an optimist," he said, years later. "I have no regrets at all. I've had quite a hard life, but it's never been boring. That's the main thing." Isabella embraces a similar philosophy. The life of an actress is tough, she has said, but well worth it when you can create something from nothing.

At the end of his career, Roberto continued to explore his "love of what happens next" in a series of documentaries about historical figures. Roberto called them "teaching films." True to his understated style, these films— *Socrates, The Age of Medici,* and *The Messiah,* to name a few— depict great moments in history with everyday gestures and almost no dramatic editing, leading *Newsweek* to call Rossellini "the Renaissance man of the modern cinema" and prompting Vincent Canby, in a June 19, 1977 *New York Times* article, to label Rossellini a genius.

"Rossellini's career," Canby wrote shortly after the director's death, "was a continuing process of discarding those tricks of hack movie making that package responses to a single work so effectively . . . . he was so zealous in his pursuit of truth in films that he followed it right out of the commercial cinema onto the public television screen, for which . . . he produced a body of work that is unique, not simply for what he was doing but for how he was doing it. It is quite conceivable that when the history of cinema's first hundred years is recollected in tranquility, say in about 150 years, Rossellini's films will be seen as among the seminal works of what, for lack of any more definite term, can be called the 'New Movie.'"

Canby seemed to believe Roberto Rossellini had outgrown his role as "the father of neorealism" and had become, even in death, a man who would continue to lead the film industry, as his techniques and philosophy of filmmaking were studied by the next generation. Roberto Rossellini would have been proud.

Isabella has followed in her father's footsteps, seeking knowledge and facing uncertainty rather than risking boredom. "My father always encouraged curiosity, and he always found an incredible pleasure in finding out, in knowledge," Isabella told Laurie Winer in a November 23, 1986 *New York Times* article. "For me, the best thing in life is to feel curiosity, to extend yourself, to fulfill your deepest curiosity, not just the gossipy part, but the knowledge to know it. To me, it's happiness.

"I miss my parents terribly," she adds, "Not only as parents, but also for their brilliance, their intelligence, their fun. The only thing I have of them is their films. . . . I can feel my father more in his films . . . and it's my way of being with him."

Isabella's father died in his apartment in Rome on June 3, 1977, of an apparent heart attack. He died in the arms of Marcella, the first of his three wives. At the time of his death, he had finally received the acknowledgement of his peers after many years of waiting.

Like her father, Isabella fought for her place in the world, even if that battle was an internal battle of her spirit. Like her father, she has never given up. And like her father, her labors have finally borne fruit. Slowly but surely, Isabella has become . . . Isabella Rossellini, the actress.

CHAPTER

6

NO ILLUSIONS

The carpet is like a racetrack, Isabella thought as she peeked around the corner. She was careful not to make a sound, stepping lightly in her favorite patent-leather shoes. Where was Robertino? She knew he was hiding around the corner. Was that the sound of him breathing? She held her breath, listening. If she could just make it down the hallway, she could hide behind the potted plant in the foyer. The high ceilings made her feel she was in a castle. And all the rooms had huge mirrors surrounded by dancing, smiling cherubs. She laughed when she first saw them, so daintily attired in olive leaves. When she danced in front of the mirrors, twirling like a ballerina, the silent cherubs kept her company, watching her every move. They always stayed at the Hotel Raphael when they were in

*Paris. It was like a second home to Isabella. Even the maids smiled
indulgently when the Rossellini children careened around the hallways,
engaged in games that went on all day long.*

*Isabella peeked around the corner. Slowly, she tiptoed down the
hall. Suddenly, she heard Robertino's footsteps bearing down on her.
She took off running, but his legs were longer! It wasn't fair, she
thought, just as her sister rounded the corner at the other end of the
hallway. Shrieking with laughter, they fell into a heap, hoping the
grown-ups wouldn't get upset.*

When she was very young, Isabella Rossellini traveled
around Europe like visiting royalty. She stayed at the best
hotels, ate at only the best restaurants, wore only the nic-
est clothes. Just as Ingrid's daydreams as a child didn't re-
flect reality, neither did Isabella's. She imagined she was a
rich gypsy.

Isabella had no way of knowing her parents were struggling to pay bills, struggling to make a living, even struggling to put food on the table. Suffering through one flop
after another, Roberto was having a difficult time convinc-
ing the "money men" to invest in his projects.

"Father was always having disasters," Isabella recalled for
Joseph Gelmis in a *Los Angeles Times* article that appeared in
May 1982. "Everything he made, he was insulted in the
press. All the films he made with my mother were not
liked.

"I loved my parents. I felt very protective toward them.
When we grew up, mother was not a star anymore. She
was considered a whore. She was considered somebody
who betrayed her husband and ruined Hollywood and all
that.

"Every time my father came out with an unsuccessful film, the critics said he was old and crazy. We felt these assaults and the intrusion of the paparazzi, very deeply, and we became protective of our parents. Every time we'd see a long lens poking out from a bush, the gang [various members of the Rossellini clan and neighborhood children] would rush out and throw stones."

Despite the underlying turmoil, in many ways, Ingrid and Roberto rose above their pain in order to give love to their children.

"What I liked best about them is probably the thing that I'm trying to imitate in my own life," Isabella said. "My father had an incredible joy. My mother, too.

"Our mother was a wise woman who kept everything in the right perspective. My father was a strong man, but he always had an affection, a tenderness, in his approach to life. You see it in all his films. My mother—she had almost an instinct for fairness in her relationships with people, everything always came out completely clearly. What's right was right and what's wrong was wrong. Sometimes, you expect a woman who has her authority to be strong. My mother wasn't like that. She was always frail—but she got her way."

When Isabella was three, her father took the entire family on the road. It was the only way he could figure out to bring in money.

Ingrid played the lead in *Joan at the Stake*, an oratorio by Paul Claudel and Arthur Honegger.

"We played in four languages in five different countries," Ingrid recalled in her autobiography.

Ingrid, Roberto, Robertino, Isabella, and Little Ingrid traveled around Europe with their nanny, all bundled into the Rolls Royce like a traveling circus—which it frequently seemed to be. Joan was performed at theaters in Paris, Milan, Stockholm, Barcelona, and London.

After seeing the show in Sweden, Stig Ahlgren wrote in the *Weekly Journal*, ". . . Ingrid Bergman is not an actress in the usual meaning. . . . To compare her with professional actresses is both mean and unjust. She travels around and she is shown for money. The promoter is Roberto Rossellini, with whom she has three children and a Rolls Royce. With art this traveling company has nothing to do. . . . Ingrid Bergman is not an actress, but a clever business woman. Coolly and soberly she has assessed the chances of making money out of her special attraction."

After *Fear* was released in 1955, Angelo Solmi wrote in *Oggi*: "[Miss Bergman and Mr. Rossellini] will either have to change their style of work radically—or retire into a dignified silence. The abyss into which Bergman and Rossellini have plunged can be measured by *Fear* . . . once the world's unquestioned number one star and successor to Greta Garbo, Miss Bergman in her latest pictures has been only a shadow of herself."

Isabella may have been a child of three, but she could feel the turmoil around her. Though she did not understand the nature of the problem, she knew her mother suffered.

Work was Ingrid's only emotional salve. Isabella was happiest when her mother was working for one simple reason: her mother was happier. Ingrid hated to be idle, cooped up in her and Roberto's apartment at 62 Via Bruno Buozzi, in Rome. If Hollywood didn't want her, she'd rather tour Europe than sit at home, staring at the walls, smoking one cigarette after another.

Isabella was the daughter of a "working mother" before the term became fashionable. Like many actresses before her, Ingrid was a feminist before her time and struggled with the guilt of juggling motherhood and work long before the issue became the subject of hundreds of articles. Without a doubt, Ingrid loved her children with a deep and abiding passion, yet she had needs of her own, apart from her roles as wife and mother. By choosing to blend career and family, Ingrid unwittingly shaped both Isabella and little Ingrid as future feminists.

"I'll never raise a family in the traditional, sociological sense," Isabella told Stan Hedman in "Ingrid Bergman's Daughter Is Here Looking at You," an article that appeared in *Sunday Woman* Magazine in September 1979. "But I don't want to say my childhood was unhappy, quite the contrary. But with a mother and a father who are roving the world all the time, I realized ordinary family life would have been unbearable.

"Happiness is not having a father sitting at home looking at TV every evening or having a mother who is changing your dresses all the time. Happiness is to share love and understanding with those who have brought you into the world. We were never children as children, if you understand what I mean. Each moment with my parents was . . . a time of intense enjoyment."

Isabella recalls "a lot of love and fun and positive feelings" in her family. But their struggle was difficult, especially when Ingrid was still considered an outcast. Her mother could no longer depend on the escape of creativity, which made the pressures in her day-to-day life with Roberto all the more difficult to contend with. Trying to raise financing for Roberto's film projects became a dismal pursuit.

Paradoxically, Ingrid worked less and less; Roberto did not want his wife to work. At first, Ingrid complied with her husband's wishes. At home in their ten-room apartment, she would usually breakfast with the children and then the nanny would take over. Ingrid would then spend hours and hours looking out the window, smoking.

The young Isabella did not know that her parents discussed bankruptcy—much less what such a cumbersome word actually meant—but she surely felt the tension and strain arising from their desperate straits. Such problems are virtually impossible to hide from children.

Roberto did not want to change his life-style. He had known a wealthy and privileged childhood and he wanted the same for his family. He could not bear the thought of not giving his children the best life possible. When the bills were just too overwhelming, Ingrid suggested they declare bankruptcy. Roberto refused.

"That life isn't worth living," Roberto told her, and, as Ingrid recalled in her autobiography, he "went on living like a millionaire." Ingrid, unlike her husband, had no qualms about being poor. A practical person—realizing Isabella, little Ingrid, and Robertino needed new clothes for school—Ingrid wrote to Joe Steel, one of her former publicity agents. "If a good picture comes up, it might be better to do that so as to buy the children new shoes." For Ingrid Bergman, that was virtually begging. She knew Joe Steel would spread the word that she needed work.

Although there were undercurrents of tension and unhappiness, Isabella recalls times of blissful enchantment with her family. They lived in a big apartment in Rome, one of the world's prettiest cities. Roberto's relatives were always about. It was very Italian—very lively, very dramatic, very emotional.

The Italian summers were an aphrodisiac to Isabella. She would play in the sun for hours, tanning to a nut-brown color, playing in the ocean near Santa Marinella, the Rossellini summer home. Whenever she wanted anything, she had only to look up and ask a servant. Both houses had servants everywhere. Isabella truly enjoyed the life-style of the rich and famous—never realizing, of course, it was an illusion.

Like her mother before her, Isabella spent hours playacting. She had an active imagination and the garden at Santa Marinella was her stage. The future thespian loved to lie under the palm trees in the backyard. The palms were mixed in with pine trees and she loved the smell of sun-warmed needles. When the sun became too hot, she would escape to the shade of one of the long verandas surrounding the house.

There was a railroad line that ran behind the house. Every day, the passengers would shout and wave towards Santa Marinella. Ingrid Bergman was considered a tourist attraction. The train conductor would sound his horn and, if Isabella was outside, she would wave at the tourists and they would wave back. She found all this attention very natural and, with hardly a thought, would go back to her playing once the train had passed.

By March 1955, Ingrid and Roberto were frequently separated. Isabella accepted her father's absences. A part of her enjoyed the quiet that filled the house when he was gone. After all, mother was always there. Yet Isabella did not remain unaware of the tensions for long. Dark silences now filled the space between Roberto and Ingrid on the increasingly rare occasions when Roberto was home. In spite of their attempts to shield their children, Roberto and Ingrid could not hide their deep unhappiness. Isabella could feel the emptiness. She knew something had changed. Too little to understand the complexity of love, she still understood that what had once been a force in their home had now retreated. She felt their dying love like a shimmery shadow she could see, but not quite grasp. She knew it was there, but she couldn't get a handle on it.

"The silences between us grew longer," Ingrid recalled in her autobiography. "The silences when I didn't dare to say anything because I would hurt his feelings. Roberto would take whatever I said, and, unhappy as he was, would make a scene about it. He liked to fight."

By January of 1956, the marriage was over. Once again, Ingrid's personal life was in a shambles, but her professional life was heating up. Roberto, his career seemingly doomed forever, struggled with feelings of loss and his fear that he would lose his children as well as his career.

Ingrid confided her fears in a letter to a friend that she included in her autobiography. "I am not afraid of being alone, but of having made four children and having them all taken away from me."

Ingrid's worst fears were eventually to come true.

CHAPTER
7

CAUGHT IN THE MIDDLE

Isabella was torn. Should she be loyal to her mother? Or loyal to her father? Night after night, she struggled with that question. She was desperate not to hurt one parent by showing favoritism to the other.

It was difficult to navigate such treacherous emotional waters. All her years could be counted on one hand, yet her parents fought over her. She didn't know what to do. She loved them both. Isabella threw herself on the bed so hard the box springs let out a groan of reproach. She stared up at the ceiling, unsure of what to do, how to react. Mother had asked them all to fill out a slip of paper with the name of the parent they'd like to live with. Tears burned in her eyes. Her mother wanted the impossible! How could she choose? She couldn't live with-

out either one. How could she not choose her mother, with her steady eyes, eyes that could sparkle with laughter in an instant. How could she not choose her father, with his overzealous bear hugs, his boisterous bedtime stories? She squeezed her eyes tight and wished she could figure out the answer. She found herself drifting off to sleep where, instead of answers, she found dreams, dreams free of loaded questions, dreams where they all lived together, just as they had in the beginning.

Isabella suffered her own wounds during her parents' divorce. Old enough to realize what was happening, but too young to make sense of it, Isabella may have felt emotionally abandoned as she was constantly shuttled from one parent to the other.

Ingrid and Roberto remained friends—at first. Roberto even insisted that Ingrid take the children. "They belong to their mother," Ingrid recalled Roberto saying to her in her autobiography. She was thrilled. She could not bear to go through another custody battle as she had with Pia. She had ultimately lost that battle after much pain, heartbreak, and separation. She had no way of knowing, however, that her happiness in gaining custody this time was premature.

The Christmas of 1956, even though they were separated, Roberto and Ingrid spent the holiday together in Rome so that the children would not be pulled in two different directions.

"I remember it all so well," Ingrid said. "Roberto lying with his head in my lap and I was laughing."

Though their happiness was illusory, at least the presents were real. Isabella loved presents. Sitting under their festive Christmas tree, she opened all her presents and even stole a sip of her mother's *glögg*—a Swedish drink made of red wine and schnapps, with nuts and raisins and cinnamon in it. She smiled happily. If this was a divorce, it was fine with her. The living room was strewn with brightly colored paper and everyone was aglow with holiday happiness and goodwill.

The real trouble began later.

When they had first decided to divorce, Roberto had asked Ingrid if she would promise never to marry again. Ingrid had laughed at the absurdity of such a request. Yet, though their marriage was essentially over, Roberto was still possessive, especially where his children were concerned. And Ingrid had no way of knowing that Roberto's penchant for theatrics would resurface when she met someone new.

Now, Ingrid was planning to marry Lars Schmidt, a Swedish theatrical producer she met after her separation from Roberto. They wanted to marry as soon as her divorce was settled. She expected it to come through in March of 1958.

"I am so happy," Ingrid wrote a friend. "And I think this time I found the right one."

Ingrid asked Isabella and little Ingrid what they thought of their mother marrying Lars. Isabella was sitting on the floor blow-drying her hair. Her mother leaned in closer, her expression earnest and serious.

"That would be great," Isabella said, according to Ingrid's autobiography.

Isabella imagined a happy home life once again. Just like the old days. She looked up at her mother, who was radiant. Isabella well understood life was better when Mama was happy.

Robertino—much his father's son—did not take the

news of Ingrid's impending marriage with the same equa-
nimity Isabella and little Ingrid had. He cried when Ingrid
told him of her plans.

Still, Ingrid hoped her new family would get along. The
next time the children flew into Paris, Lars took them all to
the park. Robertino sat up front in the car with Lars and
refused to do anything but stare glumly out the window.
Ingrid sat in back with the twins.

Finally, little Ingrid broke the silence.

"Mama? Does Lars know you want to marry him?"

"Well, I think so," Ingrid said.

"But you haven't asked him?"

"No, I haven't asked him."

"But you must ask him."

To speed matters along, little Ingrid leaned forward and
whispered into Lars's ear, "Lars would you like to marry
my mother?"

Lars was so moved by her question, he was speechless.
When he didn't speak, little Ingrid became alarmed. She
prodded him.

"Lars, my mother is still young."

Finally, Lars told little Ingrid that he would marry her
mother.

The twins were thrilled. Their brother was not.

Eventually, however, Robertino came to understand,
though Roberto never did. Just as Petter called Roberto,
"the Italian" so Roberto called Lars "the Swede." And when
Roberto finally understood that Ingrid was going to re-
marry, he was outraged. He decided he must have the
children with him.

Isabella must have felt left out when her mother did not
include the children in her wedding to Lars. Children

often feel anxious about how they will fit into their parent's new life.

Ingrid and Lars married just before Christmas in 1958 in England. Some of Lars's oldest friends from Sweden stood in as witnesses, but not one of Ingrid's children was present. By this time, Isabella had begun to accept, however sadly, that she was never to have a "normal" childhood.

Almost as soon as Ingrid said "I do," trouble with Roberto began. A bitter fight ensued for custody of their three children. The memory of the pleasant Christmas they shared after deciding to divorce seemed to fade as the battle lines were drawn. Now there were no illusions, only harsh reality.

Roberto wanted his children in Rome with him. He missed taking Robertino to the studio with him, missed Isabella's lively, energetic nature, and Little Ingrid's solemn questions about life. His pride was attacked at every turn. He couldn't sell his television documentaries—his latest project. Worst of all, he feared losing the affection of his beloved children to "the Swede." At this time, Roberto was already living with his new wife, Sonali das Gupta, her son from a previous marriage, and their newborn son. Just as he had with Ingrid, Roberto began his affair with Sonali when she was still married. When she became pregnant, she left her husband for Roberto.

At first, little Ingrid, Isabella, and Robertino were traded back and forth. The situation, however, quickly degenerated into a daily battle of wills. It got to the point that every time the children were to leave Rome to go to Ingrid, Roberto would become overwrought.

"Poor Papa, he has been crying all night," Isabella would whisper to her mother over the telephone. Already, the children were becoming pawns in a struggle between two adults, forced to deal with emotional intricacies they had no way of truly understanding.

Ingrid decided to compromise. She suggested they settle on joint custody. Roberto could see the children during the week whenever he wanted, every other weekend, and two months in the summer. That wasn't enough for Roberto. He wanted legal custody and he wanted their home in Paris, not in Choisel, about twenty-five miles outside of Paris.

Choisel, the quintessential picturesque French village, was where Lars and Ingrid had purchased a beautiful home surrounded by grand cedar trees. Isabella, especially, loved the new home, its fresh country greenery, clear skies, and quiet nights.

Roberto, who was living in a bedroom at the Hotel Raphael in Paris while trying unsuccessfully to raise money for one of his films, could not compete and knew it. Instead of slinking away in defeat, he became more determined and fought even harder. In time, Isabella would show the same strength of will.

As the struggles between Roberto and Ingrid grew, their fighting began taking a toll on the children. Isabella, normally outgoing with a sunny, vibrant personality, became jumpy. Whenever the telephone rang, she'd blurt out, "Is that the lawyer?"

Roberto was willing to fight to the finish. He claimed that Ingrid couldn't properly care for them. He brought up the fact that her name wasn't even on his son's birth certificate. He did not mention the reason—that she was still legally married to Petter Lindstrom when she gave birth to Robertino—or his role in it. Roberto made a big issue out of the fact that Ingrid did not have an extended family. He, on the other hand, had hundreds of relatives all over Rome. Roberto got his mother and his sister to sign affidavits that they would live in his house and take care of the children.

None of this surprised Ingrid. She was only too aware of how stubborn Roberto could be when he wanted something done his way. "He forces people to do what he wants them to do," she recalled in *My Story*. "He is the most stubborn human being I have ever met; but when he gets what he wants he becomes very nice."

Ingrid won the first round in the custody suit when the judge granted her temporary custody of the three children. Defeated but not broken, Roberto tried another tack. He declared that a French judge had no official jurisdiction in his case since he was Italian.

"I am an Italian citizen," he said, according to Ingrid's autobiography. "And so are the three children. I consider an Italian court decision on custody of these children more important than any ruling made in France."

Ingrid was forced to fight for her children in the Italian as well as the French courts. In spite of the problems and even as Roberto plotted his next move to win custody, Ingrid worked to get her former husband a job. She was near signing a deal with Spyros Skouras at Twentieth Century-Fox. By pulling strings, Ingrid got Spyros to offer Roberto a picture to direct. Starring Richard Burton and Joan Collins, the project was slated to start shooting in Jamaica right away. Roberto accepted the job.

Ingrid was happy, sure that Roberto's financial slump would now end and he wouldn't feel so helpless. She knew him well enough to know that once he had money coming in and was working on something challenging, he wouldn't feel so desperate about the children.

It was a sensible plan. Unfortunately, Roberto could not overcome his terrible fear of flying, a phobia he had acquired suddenly after Robertino's birth. Fox was forced to hire another director.

Once again, all Roberto's energies went into the custody battle. At the time, Isabella, little Ingrid, and Robertino were living with Ingrid and Lars at Choisel. It was not an easy time. Every day they were driven by chauffeur twenty-five miles into Paris; every night, they made the trip back. Roberto insisted it was too long a journey for the children. Ingrid and Roberto argued back and forth. Roberto wanted the children in Paris, away from Choisel and Lars.

Ingrid finally gave into Roberto's demands. She rented a permanent suite at the Hotel Raphael in Paris and hired Elena di Montis as a nanny and housekeeper to look after the children. Ingrid would stay at the apartment during the day, then return home to Choisel, and Lars, every evening.

Isabella loved the weekends, when the chauffeur would drive them to Choisel. The French countryside was like a grand adventure for her and her brother and sister, since they had always lived in cities.

Being caught in the middle of their parents' constant power struggle, however, was no adventure for the children. Roberto would have a demand. Then Ingrid. Then Roberto.

Roberto was not above grandstanding tactics. It was part of his temperament. One Friday, when the children were with him in Rome, he put them on a train to Paris. When

Ingrid went to the station to pick them up, she found her ex-husband lying in wait. For once overcoming his fear of flying, he'd flown in from Rome to beat the train because he had changed his mind—he wanted the children with him. Roberto let Ingrid take Isabella and little Ingrid. He took Robertino, telling his son only that his mother had stolen the twins. Days later, after Ingrid had managed to gather all three children under one roof, she finally sorted everything out. Crying, Robertino accused her of stealing the twins. Ingrid tried to calm her eight-year-old, but she recalls in her autobiography his question. "Mama, why didn't you steal me?"

Isabella, like her brother and sister, didn't know who was safe to love. She was fond of Lars, but she couldn't show it or it would hurt her father. Yet she didn't want to hurt her mother. Isabella became skilled at navigating the feelings of the adults in her life. She learned to think before she spoke, always careful to consider what she said to whom. One summer Lars took her swimming at the Swedish island he owned where he and Ingrid had a vacation home. Isabella was amazed to learn that many Swedes bathe naked. She had a lovely time going from the dry heat of the sauna bath into the brisk water. But still, when she went home to her father, she didn't want to seem as if she'd had too much fun, or that she liked Lars too much.

"Everyone swam naked," Isabella told Laurence Leamer in *As Time Goes By*. "But Lars went behind a rock to take off his trunks. I crept up and watched. The next time I saw my father, in order to please him I told him that Lars had a penis like a pig's tail. He laughed and laughed and every time guests would come he would make me tell the story again."

Roberto even told the children that their mother was a Protestant and they were Catholic. He told them it was a deadly sin to pray with their mother—even a prayer before dinner.

Dark circles appeared under Isabella's eyes from the strain. She had nightmares. She grew to hate the sound of a ringing telephone, always afraid that some new legal drama was about to unfold.

Ingrid decided to draw up a secret ballot. The children could vote in absolute secrecy with which parent they wanted to live. But neither Isabella nor her brother or sister could bear to make such a decision. Their parents were like night and day, but they loved them both dearly.

Ingrid was finally forced to reevaluate the situation during the Christmas of 1960. For two years, she and Roberto had fought this battle, a war that was creating emotional casualties instead of victors. The children were constantly upset and frightened. They didn't feel they had a safe haven.

Christmas was particularly difficult. Ingrid had secretly spirited her children to Norway, where Lars was producing a play. She knew that had she asked Roberto, he would have objected, so she simply took them without asking. In Rome, Roberto was nearing hysteria. Then, by chance, Ingrid read a news item describing a tragedy that had befallen a friend that Christmas. Eduardo De Filippo, an Italian actor she and Roberto knew, was on vacation when his only child fell ill with a strange disease and died twenty-four hours later. Ingrid was deeply affected by this tragedy. Like any good actress, she had the ability to empathize with the plight of others. She began to think of her ex-husband, childless, in Rome. By New Year's Eve, Ingrid was deeply pensive. She looked back on the year.

"To whom have I brought happiness?" Ingrid, in *My Story*, recalls having asked herself at that time. "What have I done wrong? Next year, can I be kinder and nicer? And all the time the bells are caroling peace and goodwill across the countryside. And here I was fighting over the three children as I'd fought over Pia."

Ingrid called Roberto. "All right. You can have the children. I give up. You can have the children in Italy and bring them up there. I'm bringing them down to you right away."

Isabella, little Ingrid, and Robertino didn't understand the sudden change, but they knew they were going back to Italy, for good.

"Mother and Father were fighting so hard over who would have us that Mother finally gave in, knowing it was terribly painful for us to go through the arguing," Isabella told Laurence Leamer.

Even though Ingrid's lawyer told her she would undoubtedly win the custody case, she had had enough.

"I'm not going to go on," she told her lawyer. "I'm not coming here any more to go through the law courts. I'm giving Roberto the children." Surprisingly, Isabella, little Ingrid, and Robertino did not live with their father. Though Roberto had fought so hard to win the children, he didn't live with them. He lived across the street with his new wife and young son. Isabella and her brother and sister lived with their nanny in a big apartment down the street from the one their father shared with his new family.

Isabella felt a need, years later, to defend her mother's actions, just as she used to defend her mother from the photographers hiding in the bushes when she was a little girl.

"My mother felt terribly guilty that she had to be away

from us," said Isabella. "She shouldn't have, because we didn't suffer from the divorce. Even when she wasn't home, I knew she loved me."

Perhaps it is that generosity of spirit that is part of Isabella's gift to her parents. And yet, David Lynch saw something different in her. When he first met her, he saw "some sort of sadness, a mystery, something I didn't understand."

No matter how mature young Isabella was, or how much insight she gained as a young woman, she must have felt deep pain and sadness when her father and mother divorced, and the times they shared became special events rather than something she could count on every day.

For the next twelve years, Ingrid commuted from Choisel to Rome to see her children. A new nanny, Argenide Pascolini, became the children's new day-to-day "mother." Isabella, Ingrid, and Robertino tried to adjust to their new life.

"It wasn't lonely," Isabella insisted to Alice Steinbach in "On Her Own," an article that appeared in the November 1985 issue of the *Saturday Review*. "You know, people in America live very isolated lives in their homes and the family relationship is not as extended as in Latin countries. I have my aunt, my cousins, living next door. Most of the time in Italy, we are in the streets. You just go home to sleep. I liked having the children's house, because we could make noise."

When both parents were away, which was usually the case, the governess kept a strict account of the misdeeds of her charges and reported back to Ingrid and Roberto.

"She would send mother a written report on our behavior and we'd sit down and discuss it," Isabella told Lawrence Eisenberg in a February 1983 *Cosmopolitan* article. "There was no immediate punishment or reward, just a lot of talk with both my father and mother, and I think I still, every time I have to make a decision, I imagine a discussion with both of them.

"There was no hostility or fear in it for me, as I think there are in so many cases where there are divorces and remarriages and stepbrothers and sisters," Isabella said. "I didn't differentiate, even in my feelings, between my full and half and stepbrothers and sisters. Father was an incredible man, both intellectual and emotional at the same time, very original. Mama's strength was her capacity to be direct. She had terrific instincts for dealing with children.

"My mother's ability to be a good mother has been questioned throughout her life. This is very painful. We were always so, very, very close."

But it was a hard-won closeness. After six years of living primarily in Rome with her father, Isabella's relationship with her mother was strained. Their relationship was resurrected only after Isabella was diagnosed with a painful, serious illness, which had a life-threatening cure. Only then did Isabella became the recipient of her parents' undivided attention. Hollywood beckoned Ingrid from across ·the ocean with impressive offers, but Ingrid ignored the temptation. For nearly two years, Ingrid and Roberto helped their thirteen-year-old daughter endure treatments for her potentially crippling illness. Nothing else existed. For while Roberto and Ingrid had always loved their children with a deep, abiding passion, their love was sometimes more ethereal than finite, and their children—because of the circumstances of their birth and the resulting stresses

Ingrid and Roberto were subjected to—were sometimes shortchanged. Now, Roberto and Ingrid put aside their personal needs and lived only for their child.

It was a time of great happiness for Isabella, in spite of her illness, and one that bonded mother and daughter for life.

CHAPTER 8

TO STAND ALONE

Isabella stretched her hands toward the ceiling, trying to get some relief. Her back hurt and the pain wouldn't stop, no matter what she did. For months she had tried to ignore the dull ache in the middle of her back. She figured she had been climbing too many trees.

One by one, Isabella watched her classmates leave the doctor's office. Soon it would be her turn. She sat up as straight as possible as she waited. Anyone who wanted to be on the gymnastics team had to have a physical examination. Isabella didn't mind at all. It was a great excuse to miss class.

Finally, it was her turn. The doctor examined her and then he listened to her breath, his stethoscope resting lightly on her back. She could feel his hands, cool and comforting on her skin.

"Has your back been hurting?" the doctor asked her.

Isabella, surprised, nodded and wondered why he asked that. When she saw the look in his eyes, she wondered if it was anything serious.

———

In 1965, Isabella was diagnosed as having scoliosis—an abnormal S-shaped curvature of the spine that could get increasingly worse over time. If her condition was left untreated, Isabella's sturdy frame could begin to twist into that of a hunchback. The only chance of escaping such a fate was to undergo a dangerous, six-hour operation.

Ingrid heard the news in Paris and caught the first plane to Rome. When the doctor explained Isabella's condition, she peered at her daughter's back, lightly tracing the curvature of her spine with her fingertips.

"Yes," Ingrid recalled in her autobiography with Alan Burgess. "I can see her spine is not straight, it has a slight S-shape. But surely that isn't serious."

Quite the contrary. Isabella's scoliosis was termed "galloping." The doctors wanted to operate immediately. Ingrid and Roberto, however, insisted on getting several other medical opinions. They wanted to avoid subjecting Isabella to a risky operation before they explored other options. First, they tried more conservative treatments, such as having their daughter wear special shoes that made one hip higher than the other, and having her wear a supportive leather girdle. Nothing worked. By the time Ingrid and Roberto took Isabella back to the doctor, her condition had deteriorated.

Roberto, Ingrid, and Isabella went to Florence. Once again, they met with one specialist after another, who took X-rays of Isabella's spine from every conceivable angle.

The process seemed endless but the final diagnosis was still a shock. When a specialist read the X-rays, he said: "It could be the beginning of a hunchback." Isabella was too stunned to speak.

"I did feel—well, deformed is a very heavy word, but maybe just a little deformed," Isabella told Alexandra Witchel in *Elle* magazine in January of 1986.

An operation was the only possible alternative. Roberto told the doctor they would have to think about it and hustled his ex-wife and his daughter out into the fresh air. The streets of Florence were dazzling but Isabella, Ingrid, and Roberto were silent, each pondering the future.

It was Isabella who would make the decision. She told her mother to call the doctor and schedule the operation.

The decision was the easy part. Before the doctors would perform the operation, Isabella's spine had to be pulled as straight as possible. Over several weeks, Isabella was "stretched." It was the most painful thing Isabella had ever experienced.

Isabella was stretched. Then she was stretched more. It was so painful she thought the doctors were going to pull her apart. The doctors did not use any anesthetic, for if they anesthetized her, they wouldn't know how much it was hurting and consequently when to stop the stretching.

"They stretched me on a 'torture bed' until I fainted," Isabella retold David Hutchings in an August 2, 1982 *People* magazine article.

Ingrid and Roberto listened to their child screaming and stared at each other. They were now living a parent's nightmare—knowing your child is in pain and being powerless to do anything about it. It seemed to last forever. Finally, Isabella's screams turned to whimpers.

When Ingrid was allowed back in the room, Isabella was covered in plaster from her neck to her hips. Ingrid had never seen her rosy-cheeked Isa so pale.

"Mama, Mama, it hurts so much," she whispered, the lilt gone from her voice.

Ingrid held Isabella's hand while they waited for the plaster to dry.

The first stretching was a terrible ordeal, but Isabella recovered quickly. Within days, she was eating and laughing, holding court from her hospital bed.

At home, all the Rossellini relatives were solicitous of Isabella. After all, she was soon to endure a frightening operation, so it was only right that she be pampered and spoiled. Ingrid had special dresses made to cover the heavy cast and Isabella wore them with pride. She tried not to think about the next stretching, but, before she knew it, it was time. Once again, Isabella headed back to Florence with her parents. She had to kneel on the car seat for the entire journey. She couldn't sit naturally because of the cast.

The second stretching was even worse. Isabella cried. She screamed. After they stretched her on the "torture rack," the doctors encased her in plaster again. She had to endure three stretchings in all before she could have the operation.

Finally, the doctors decided she was ready. There was only one problem: Scaglietti Hospital did not have enough blood in their blood banks for Isabella's operation. Each patient was limited to a certain amount and Isabella would require many times that for her procedure.

It was up to Isabella's mother to collect the needed blood. Ingrid went to everyone in the family, as well as

Isabella's schoolmates. Everyone offered to donate their blood to help Isabella. Ingrid then took the collected blood to Florence.

The operation was lengthy. The actual surgery was a painstaking and delicate process. The surgeon made an incision in Isabella's leg from the knee down to her foot, cutting out about a third of her shin bone. (Since Isabella was so young, the shin bone would grow back, though her leg would be in a cast for six months.) The shin was then sliced into small slivers, the size of matches. The surgeon then made a cut down the length of Isabella's back and delicately placed the bone slivers between each disc to prevent the spine from curving back to its original position. The surgeon had to use Isabella's own bone tissue to ensure that her immune system didn't reject it as a foreign entity.

Out in the waiting room, Roberto did crossword puzzles. He didn't want to think, so he spent hours concentrating on word games. Ingrid smoked one cigarette after another until she could stand it no longer. She disappeared into the bathroom. Finally, Roberto grew worried. Where was she?

Ingrid was washing her hair. She always washed her hair when she was upset. It took her mind off the agony at hand.

After six hours, Dr. Ponti, the surgeon who performed the operation, appeared at the door to the waiting room.

Ingrid rushed ahead to the recovery rooms, leaving Roberto and Dr. Ponti behind. She rushed into the first open door she saw. All she saw was a body lying on a bed, a mass of bandages. The girl was sleeping, her face turned away. As told in her autobiography, Ingrid promptly became hysterical.

"What have you done to my child? You've shortened her. Good heavens, what have you done?"

Dr. Ponti silenced her. "You are in the wrong room," he told her. "This is not your child."

Dr. Ponti led Roberto and Ingrid to Isabella, who was pale and connected to countless intravenous tubes. She was not awake yet. Both Ingrid and Roberto started sobbing. They walked beside her bed, clutching her limp hand, as the nurses rolled her back to her room. Isabella was still sleeping off the anesthetic when one of the nurses began to slap her face.

Ingrid yelled at the nurse to stop hitting her daughter. Roberto told her it was routine. Isabella must wake up. But Ingrid couldn't take it anymore. She fainted, falling into Roberto's arms.

Ingrid was installed in the room next to Isabella's. Roberto took care of them both that night. Isabella woke up once in the middle of the night and she tried to talk, but Roberto couldn't understand what she was saying.

"Belfagor. Belfagor," she said. Roberto finally realized that it was the name of her favorite television show. She'd missed it because of her operation. Roberto promised his daughter she could see it in the morning if she went back to sleep.

The days ahead were filled with pain. Isabella showed a courageous spirit for one so young. Her mother's eyes were constantly red from crying, though she tried to be stoic in front of her daughter.

"Mother, don't cry so much," Isabella told her. "I'm not sorry this has happened to me. In the future, when people talk about pain, I will know what it means. It might help me to help others who suffer."

Ingrid spent every day and every night next to Isabella. It was the first time in Isabella's life that her mother had been so available to her.

"That period changed my perception of her," Isabella told Laurence Leamer in *As Time Goes By*, a biography of Ingrid Bergman.

"Until then I was very much my father's daughter. But it established the relationship that we had afterwards. I don't know if she regretted that she hadn't spent more time with us. She did always come and visit."

Isabella was transported back to Rome in grand style. She rode home flat on her back in an ambulance, the siren blaring. She stayed on her back for six months, her body encased in plaster.

"The bad part was the pain and all that, but most of it was kind of interesting," Isabella told Lawrence Eisenberg in the February 1983 *Cosmopolitan* article, "Bella Bella Isabella." "For example, growing up in Italy—a highly verbal and intellectual country—and in a family that's very talented, you think that the thing you want most is your brain and your capacity for talking. But once you lose your capacity for walking or standing up, you know the thing you want most is walking, and it really gives you a different attitude toward life's prospects."

At home, her parents gave Isabella a gift she cherished—Ferdinando, a dachshund. He kept her company during the eighteen months it took her to recover, rarely leaving her side. Isabella spent hours playing with Ferdinando and listening to Beatles records.

Isabella was overjoyed when the first six months were up. Never had time passed so slowly than the time she had spent listening to her friends outside playing in the streets while she was trapped indoors. Now, after she went back to Florence and the doctors outfitted her with a brand-new mini cast, she would be able to go back to school! She could even go dancing.

Isabella was past the first hurdle. The rest of her recovery would not be as painful or as lonely.

"We decided that if she could get through scoliosis as well as she did," Isabella's twin told John Skow in a May 2, 1983 *Time* magazine article, "then she could get through anything."

After a total of eighteen months, the big day arrived. Isabella's cast was removed. She pressed her hands against her ears to shut out the noise of the electric saw. For the first time in over a year and a half, she felt fresh air against her skin. All of her senses were alive. When Dr. Ponti told her she could stand up, Isabella didn't believe him. She was afraid she wouldn't be strong enough on her own.

Isabella was taken to the pool in a wheelchair. Dr. Ponti wanted her to go swimming so she could immediately experience ease and fluidity in her movements after so many months of clumsy immobility. Isabella swam around the pool like a little otter. Back in Rome, the apartment was filled with life and laughter as the "new" Isabella was unveiled. Isabella was strong and healthy once again.

CHAPTER
9

REBEL WITHOUT A CAUSE

Isabella tried to look nonchalant as she glanced down the street. Standing below the movie marquee, she read the title: Open City. It was the film that had made her father famous. Should she or shouldn't she? Her father had been explicit: she was not allowed to see his movies. Isabella had different ideas. She had a right to make up her own mind! If she wanted to see her father's movies, who was he to stop her? After all, the rest of the world could see them! Was she to be the only one excluded? She looked down the street again, scanning the faces. Good, she thought. The coast is clear. Only strangers jostled past her as she stood outside the small movie house not far from home. More people filed past her into the dark theater. She must decide. She hated to go against her father's wishes, but she wanted to see for herself *why his movies caused such a furor. She had read dozens—no, hundreds—of articles about him in various newspapers and magazines, yet he wouldn't let her see the films everyone was still talking about! It wasn't fair, she thought. That did it. Her mother always stressed fairness above all else. She made up her mind and resolutely marched into the theater, one foot in front of the other. The darkness was a shield; no one would recognize her. Her father seemed to know everyone in Rome—everyone in Italy for that matter. She could just hear one of his friends casually remarking, "I saw one of the twins in the theater the other day, watching your film. Do you always let your daughters go to movies all alone?" Isabella smiled to herself, imagining her father's outrage at her flagrant misbehavior. She found a seat and snuggled into the velvet cushions as the house lights grew dim, watching intently as the credits for* Open City *began. Like her mother so many years before, Isabella sat mesmerized by her father's art, in which his spirit could so clearly be felt.*

The rebellious spirit of Isabella Rossellini flourished at an early age. It is a characteristic that still defines her. As a child, she loved to laugh, loved to dare her friends into mischief, loved to take risks. As an adult, she still loves to laugh, still loves to take risks. Isabella was a teenager— practically grown up, in her mind—when she decided to defy her father and see his movies. Roberto Rossellini probably did not want his children exposed to the violent scenes in his World War II trilogy, but Isabella wanted to be a part of his artistic life. She was proud of him as a man and as a father, but especially as an artist. And if she had to defy him to indulge that love, she would.

As an adult, it frustrated Isabella when young people didn't know of her father's films, or worse, who he was.

Once Isabella had a not-so-amusing encounter with a teenager who told her how sorry she was about the terrible way Isabella's father had been killed and spat upon.

"I told her she was thinking about Mussolini," Isabella told William Wolf in "Heiress to Greatness," an article that appeared in *New York* magazine in August 1982. "My father told me that in Hollywood, Samuel Goldwyn always called him Mussolini. That's terrible for someone who was a symbol of anti-Fascism in Italy."

Isabella adored her father, but she also railed against him. In many ways, Roberto was the stereotypical Italian father; proud and loving, but also domineering. So Isabella did what she thought was right; she rebelled.

"I had terrible arguments with my father," Isabella told Lawrence Eisenberg in "Bella Bella Isabella." "My twin sister Isotta was always very shy and I wasn't, so I was the one who had to break the news to him about going out with boys and falling in love with boys, and it's hard for fathers, especially if they're Italian. He probably had a point, it's true, because I was supposed to be home at nine and I was always home at ten-thirty or eleven. But he overreacted to things that weren't so bad . . . that's one of the reasons I moved to the U.S."

But that move was years away. As a teenager, Isabella frequently clashed with her strong-minded father. After Isabella's bout with scoliosis, Ingrid returned to her life with Lars, and Isabella had to deal with her father alone until Pia Lindstrom, surprisingly, came to live with the three Rossellini children after Isabella's grandmother on her father's side passed away.

With Pia's arrival, some of the friction between father

and daughter abated, since Pia acted as a nanny and was much more permissive (more American) than Roberto.

Like Isabella, it took Pia many years to step from her mother's shadow and find her way in the world. Mirroring Isabella, but in reverse, Pia started out as an actress and ended up as a journalist.

After one failed marriage just out of college, Pia ended up staying in Paris where she spent a lot of time with her mother and Lars, unconsciously trying, perhaps, to regain the mother she'd lost at the age of thirteen. Pia found the old adage "you can't go home again" to be true. She still felt at loose ends so when Ingrid asked her if she wanted to help take care of Isabella, little Ingrid, and Robertino, she agreed.

For the next few years, she was surrogate mother to the three teenagers. She couldn't go home again but she could still try to enjoy the family life she had missed as a child.

"I stayed there for about three years with them," Pia said. "Mother sent me the money. I paid the salaries, and I took them to the dentist, and horseback riding, and for lessons. I took Robertino skiing and organized the family."

How ironic that Pia, the daughter Ingrid abandoned for her Italian lover, should take part in raising the children from that union. The irony was not lost on Pia.

"Sometimes I'd say, 'This is ridiculous! What am I doing here? What would my father think?' I'm sure my father did not think well of it: he must have thought it was a terrible thing for me to go to Italy and live with those three children. Anyway I did it and it did strike me sometimes as very peculiar."

Pia returned to America after her three-year sojourn, having helped Isabella navigate her early teenage years with her strict father. To this day, Pia and Isabella remain close. They both live in New York City, where Pia works as a television journalist. The two visit often and recently Pia interviewed Isabella for a long news segment in which they discussed a retrospective of Roberto Rossellini's work.

As soon as Pia left, Roberto tried to resume the role of a strict disciplinarian. Isabella refused to let her father run her life.

By the time Isabella and her sister Ingrid reached their late teens, Roberto—like most fathers—found himself even more protective. He frequently became so unsettled by all the young men calling on "his" girls that Isabella had to phone her mother and ask her to talk to him. Roberto was more permissive with Robertino. Isabella's brother, almost two years older than his sisters, was constantly running around with his friends, who included Princess Caroline of Monaco and others. Isabella railed against the double standard but she could not change the fact her father was more protective of his daughters than his son.

Isabella was now a self-determined, socially aware woman. Ditto for her twin, Ingrid, who would grow up to be a scholar. By the time she was eighteen, Isabella became an avowed feminist, working long hours to promote reform in areas such as abortion, wife abuse, and divorce. She frequently worked late at night, attending rallies, handing out pamphlets, and counseling victims of abuse.

"I do have very strong sympathies for feminist issues," Isabella told Alice Steinbach years later in "On Her Own," a December 1985 *Saturday Review* article. "They concern equal rights, abortion, and divorce. In Italy, we had a very strong struggle for abortion and divorce and I was very active at the time working for more liberal laws."

As well as being an avid feminist, Isabella also launched

a fledgling career while still in high school—one of several she would pursue before finding her true vocation. She'd shown an early flair for design while working in the costume department on all of her father's films. By the age of seventeen, she was dubbed one of Italy's most promising young textile designers, and was awarded several prestigious honors. The world of design, however, did not inspire Isabella. It would be more than a decade before she would discover what did evoke her passion. At the time, however, she passionately wanted independence. Roberto, on the other hand, still wanted his daughter home early. And he wanted a say in her life. Isabella rebelled and eventually moved to New York City.

It's no surprise that Isabella was chafing to be on her own. By the time she was nineteen, she wanted—like every other girl her age—more freedom from the confines of her family. Much as she loved them, she wanted to forge her own identity. She decided she would go to America and find work.

CHAPTER
10

THE AMERICANIZATION
OF ISABELLA

The brilliant lights of Rome disappeared as Isabella stared out the window. "Twenty thousand feet and climbing," the captain announced. Isabella had butterflies in her stomach. She didn't want to admit she was nervous about her destination—New York City. She swallowed hard, then looked out the window again. Rome was nothing but a point of light in the distance. Suddenly, her skin felt prickly. Was she making a mistake? What was she doing, hurtling through the sky, away from all the people she loved most in the world? Deep down, she knew her father was dismayed. He had never forgiven America for what it had done to her mother, and to him. He wanted her to stay in Italy. But she had suffocated there. . . . She forced herself to breathe deeply, willing herself to be calm. Her face, she saw in the diffuse *reflection of the plane window, was surprisingly serene. No one would ever guess she was off on the biggest adventure of her life. She had no idea what awaited her in America. She had no idea nothing would ever be the same.*

It was Isabella's first big adventure. She was fueled, like so many young women, by a desire to create her own life. And, like all women who take charge of their destinies, she must have been frightened yet exhilarated at the prospect of change.

No doubt, exhilaration had won out over fear, giving her the strength to take those first steps away from the life she knew so well, towards the life she would create for herself in the States.

All her life, Isabella was, admittedly, too playful and too given to fantasy to bloom under the strict discipline common in European schools. By the time she left Rome to live in America, she was ripe for the relaxed, creative atmosphere she found at New York City's New School for Social Research, where she took classes. The atmosphere inspired her to work harder than she had ever worked.

Isabella was also ripe for living her own life, away from her strong, volatile, overprotective father. Isabella excelled as she slowly took control of her own destiny, a process that would last much of the next ten years.

"I came to the United States to work," she said in a February 7, 1981 *New York Times* article. She began her new life by teaching Italian to American students at the New School. This enabled her to polish her English, important because, "In Italy, you're told if you learn English, your future will be assured."

In spite of an unremarkable earlier scholastic performance, Isabella has been, without question, an achiever as an adult. After her stint at the New School, she happened upon a job that tested her resources. In addition to teaching English, Isabella also did translations. One translation happened to be for an Italian journalist living in New York. Impressed with her language skills, he helped her get a job answering telephones at the New York bureau for RAI-TV, the Italian state television system.

That didn't last long. At record speed, Isabella was booted upstairs. She started working as a reporter, doing celebrity interviews on a show called "L'Altra Domenica" ("The Other Sunday")—the Italian television version of America's "Saturday Night Live." Isabella, not her mother, was now tracked by cameras.

Crisscrossing the country with her own camera crew, the rising star interviewed such celebrities as Muhammed Ali, Woody Allen, Barbra Streisand, and Martin Scorcese.

The show proved to be a springboard. During a trip to Italy, she was approached with yet another television offer, a chance to join a comedy show called "Papocchio" ("The Week That Was"). She jumped at the opportunity. Once again, Isabella found she had the Midas touch. "Papocchio" was a nationwide success in Italy.

"I was something of a star," Isabella told Bruce Cook in "Isabella Rossellini: A Rose Who Has Known Thorns," in the *Chicago Tribune* article published on November 28, 1985. "The program became very successful and I did it for years. It was a strange sort of journalism, mixing reportage with comedy. I always tried to make my segments as funny as I could. I like fun. When the show was cancelled, I tried being a serious journalist for two years and I wasn't happy. I don't think I'm a serious journalist because I'm not very serious.

"If I had to be remembered for one thing, I hope it would be as a funny person."

The young journalist stayed with RAI-TV for four years. She still talks with pleasure about her days as a roving reporter, learning the tricks of the trade in the world of television journalism and using them like a pro. When she wanted to interview a certain celebrity and that particular celebrity was skittish, she wouldn't necessarily disclose the entire truth about her show. "Sometimes I didn't say my program was experimental," she said. "I just said, 'Italian television,' which wasn't a lie, but it just wasn't very precise. It was Italian television, only it was like 'Sesame Street.'"

The Italian celebrity status she was fast gaining did not blind Isabella to the irony of working as a journalist, considering the abuse both her parents had received at the hands of the press. "I heard so many complaints from mother and father," Isabella told Joseph Gelmis in a May 23, 1982 *Los Angeles Times* article, "A Child of the Movies Makes Movies." "One of the worst things my family had to go through was that you meet a person for ten, fifteen minutes and then the person writes about your life and says how awful and rotten you are. That was the hard part of being a journalist [for me]. Sometimes, [I felt I was] interfering in people's private lives."

RAI-TV brought Isabella to the Italian people. It also brought her to Martin Scorcese.

Scorcese had just directed *The Last Waltz* in 1978. "I admired him so much as a director that I was intimidated," Isabella told Lawrence Eisenberg, her words reminiscent of the way Ingrid Bergman was inspired when she first experienced the magic of Roberto Rossellini's filmmaking.

"I don't think it was my best interview. Marty is such a strange type. He speaks very fast, like a machine gun. He moves like a monkey, so fast—almost like a squirrel. I was very surprised. I didn't expect that at all. His films are so important that I really expected a big, tall man, completely intellectual. Instead, he looked like a punk rock-'n' roller. I liked him. A lot."

The interview led to courtship and the courtship led to the altar. They were married in September of 1979. It was a beautiful, Italian wedding held in the outskirts of Rome. The press was barred.

Unfortunately, the marriage was not destined to last. Almost from the time of their honeymoon, the newlyweds had to endure separations imposed by their careers. Isabella was also under a great deal of emotional strain; her mother was undergoing treatments for cancer. Five years earlier, in 1974, Ingrid had been diagnosed with breast cancer. Her struggle with the disease had grown worse. Isabella visited her as often as possible in London, where Ingrid was living.

Isabella was also still mourning her father, who had died in 1977. When asked by Eisenberg whether there were similarities between her father and her new husband, Isabella said, "I'm fascinated with bright men, that's the only thing they have in common. They're very different and their films are very different."

For Isabella, the romance was serious from the beginning.

"I had boyfriends before Marty . . . but I never felt so strongly about anyone. I talked to my mother about it. She told me I ought to get married to Marty if he was deeply moving to me."

Isabella and Marty shared the world of filmmaking, but just as Ingrid learned with Roberto, filmmaking does not a marriage make. Their relationship, however, helped shape the artist Isabella was to become.

"Marty taught me about film and the process of creativity, how an artist works," Isabella explained to Eisenberg.

"Basically our marriage was about films. It's very hard for me to talk about Marty and not talk about film. He can talk about history, human feeling, anything, but always in relation to film. When I married him, I always knew the story was going to be very passionate, very intense, but we were going to burn out. Marty burns things out. It's very much a part of the way he lives, the way he expresses life in his art."

In 1982, near the end of their marriage, Isabella's modeling career began to heat up. Personal unhappiness was followed by professional success.

"I was only modeling two months at the time we separated, so the modeling didn't end the marriage," Isabella told Eisenberg. "But Marty did have a hard time with my modeling because in modeling there's sex appeal and a sex image around the model. That was hard for him to deal with. It was wonderful for me to be a model, an emotion that was making him nervous."

Still, it was Scorcese who helped Isabella embrace her career.

"I was very rigid, very severe," Isabella told William Wolf in an August 2, 1982 *New York* magazine article, referring to the time before she met Marty. "I used to feel you shouldn't relate to beauty, because you just create conflicts in people. But Marty helped loosen me up."

Roberto Rossellini and Martin Scorcese may have been very different, as Isabella said, but they did have at least one thing in common. Both detested the idea of Isabella becoming an actress. When it became clear she was going to follow in her mother's footsteps, Scorcese disapproved. Though Isabella's father was no longer alive when Isabella's acting career began, he might have disapproved as well. He had always discouraged her from choosing that career. He thought actors had hard lives, and wanted to spare Isabella the rejection inherent in the profession. And he did not want her hurt the way her mother had been hurt by Hollywood. "In this area my father was very repressive," Isabella told David Hutchings in an August 2, 1982 *People* magazine article.

Isabella admits that her husband had a significant amount of trepidation—he had married a television journalist, not an actress. "He said," as Isabella told Eisenberg, "Oh my God, an actress. Deliver me from an actress."

Just as she had rebelled at thirteen and gone to see her father's films, so Isabella began to rebel against the expectations of others. She struggled to stand on her own, to unearth, deep inside her heart, what it was she wanted to do.

Helpless to repair their crumbling marriage, Isabella continued to work. Like her mother, Isabella found work a solace during hard times.

When Paolo and Vittorio Taviani, two brothers who were award-winning Italian filmmakers, saw Isabella on Italian television, they remembered the days when they worked as Roberto Rossellini's assistants, many years before. Back then, Isabella was a gangly young girl, not the five-foot-eight beauty she had become. When they saw her improvisational work in "Papocchio," they thought:

Wouldn't it be nice to have Isabella appear in one of their movies?

Isabella went to Italy to make *The Meadow* in 1981 when her marriage to Scorcese was nearly finished. Three years later, Isabella said she regretted their break-up. "Marty and I had a wonderful marriage," she told Phyllis Battelle in "Like Mother, Like Daughter?" a 1985 *Ladies Home Journal* article. "If I had been older, wiser and calmer we might still be together. . . . But it broke up because we had a tremendous amount of stress. Mother was dying of cancer in London. She was very brave about it but she was in great pain before she died. It's strange that sometimes sorrow brings people together and sometimes it doesn't. You become closer if you're solid, strong, and capable. But if you're not, and I was not, it can separate you. I panicked and decided it would be better not to be married."

Yet just months after her divorce, Isabella married someone else. She met Jonathan Wiedemann, an aspiring director. By the time Isabella and the tall, red-haired Texan married, she was already wearing maternity clothes.

"I have divorced Martin Scorcese because he wanted me to spend life between the cookstove and the kids," Isabella was quoted in *Time* magazine in March 1983. "With my new husband, it is different."

Isabella and Jon, five years her junior, met on a modeling shoot in Mexico. Jonathan had recently graduated *magna cum laude* from Harvard. He was also earning money as a model while pursuing a master's degree in filmmaking at New York University. If Martin Scorcese brought an almost feral intensity to his marriage with Isabella, Jonathan Wiedemann brought comparative tranquility.

"Jon seemed very calm, serene, balanced, healthy, and

fun," Isabella told Phyllis Battelle in the November 1985 *Ladies Home Journal* article. "I am sometimes very impetuous, then I suffer afterward. My mother used to say that having fun doing something is an indication that it's right. Well, Jon's an explorer at heart and I was drawn to him because he took fun vacations, river rafting and mountain climbing, all those fascinating things I'd never done before. Then I couldn't share those things with him because I became pregnant."

Jonathan recalled their beginning to John Skow of *Time* magazine. "After she and Marty split up, we became much closer. We fell in love, started a family and got married. I guess we mixed up the order a bit."

Even though Isabella's second marriage ended in divorce, she is proud of the fact she had Elettra-Ingrid Rossellini Wiedemann when she did. Isabella does not believe in the way Americans pursue their careers, as if nothing else matters.

"My sense of identity isn't bound up in my career," she told John Skow of *Time* magazine. "Americans tend to be like greyhounds, running all the time. I enjoy being in the race, too, but suddenly I'm struck by the sun and decide, if I have enough money, to do nothing for six months. That's very European. I don't fear the loss of success."

Isabella's balanced attitude comes, no doubt, in part from witnessing firsthand the ephemeral nature of success. Her mother was the queen of Hollywood until the scandal. Her father was Europe's brightest new director until the press dubbed him a Svengali. No wonder Isabella feels capable of distancing herself from the rat race with a spontaneous, six-month vacation. She knows only too well that a career can disappear in an instant, regardless of how many years were spent creating it.

At an age when many American women are getting married for the first time in their late twenties and early thirties, Isabella already had two divorces behind her. The similarities to Ingrid Bergman, whose three marriages all ended in divorce, are obvious. It is a pattern that clearly worries Isabella.

"Mother had longer marriages," Isabella told Alice Steinbach of the *Saturday Review*. "So that's something that bothers me. I'm kind of at the interrogation mark in my life. I don't know which way it will go."

It doesn't take long for Isabella to see the humor in the situation, a perspective that is one of her great strengths. "I'm very romantic," she told Battelle. "And how do I express my romanticism? By getting married so often."

When her marriage to Jon came to an end, Isabella's career took off when she was cast in *White Nights*. She played opposite Mikhail Baryshnikov—called "Misha" by his friends—and the stage was set for another romance. It was only after Isabella's second marriage broke up that Isabella and Misha began to see each other.

"If you ask me whether Misha broke up my marriage, the answer is no, that didn't happen," Isabella told Battelle. "People said I was in love with Misha from the first time I saw him. I understand why they would say that. Just look at him. He's not only charming and beautiful, he's intelligent, brilliant!"

Isabella loathes talking about her personal life. She can speak about her films, the characters she inhabits, with ease, but she rebels against revealing her innermost feelings, perhaps in part because she is still struggling to sort them out herself.

"I find it very hard to talk about my husbands and lovers in rational terms," she told Battelle. "I'm not hiding anything, I wish I did have the answers to my feelings, my life would be much easier. The only person I can really talk to about these problems is my psychiatrist. And together, even we haven't figured it all out."

After her second marriage broke up and Isabella became a single mother, she struggled with her own sense of maternal guilt—something her own mother had struggled with most of her life. Isabella discovered that in many ways, the role of mother is much more difficult than that of daughter.

"My mother felt terribly guilty that she had to be away from us," Isabella told Steinbach. "She shouldn't have, because we didn't suffer from the divorce. Even when she wasn't home, I always knew she loved me."

Like all working mothers, Isabella takes it one day at a time. She hopes her experiences with her own mother will lead her in the right direction.

"I attended an acting seminar once that was absolutely fascinating," Isabella told Battelle. "Each day a topic would be picked and the students took turns giving their experiences. One day the subject was our relationships with our mothers. When my turn came, everybody was expecting a dramatic story because, of course, they knew all about my mother. I didn't have a big, sad story at all. The dramatic stories came from the students whose mothers had stayed home for the sake of their children instead of having fulfilling careers. Those kids said they were made to feel so guilty . . . a sort of transferred guilt, because they'd kept their mothers from doing what they really wanted to do. I so wish my mother were alive so I could ease her pain by telling her that."

Isabella pays a homage, of sorts, to her mother by being the kind of mother Ingrid might have wanted to be. Isabella always takes her young daughter on location with her. Isabella's is usually the first face Elettra sees every morning. Today, many years after the death of her mother, Isabella has come to personify the kind of mother that Ingrid wanted, but never managed, to be. And as an artist, Isabella, in her climb to stardom, is slowly gaining the same foothold in the acting world that her mother occupied so steadfastly for so many years. Unlike her mother, however, Isabella has her daughter at her side.

Isabella has yet to marry again, but she's been in love with one man for the past three years: David Lynch, the iconoclastic director who enabled her to give such a riveting performance in *Blue Velvet*.

It is a seemingly unlikely, but enduring union.

Lynch, who is six years Isabella's senior, also has two marriages behind him. It is probably the bond of creativity Isabella and David share that has kept their love alive and vibrant. They both see creation, and art, as a way of life.

Like Isabella's father, Lynch was always drawn to the worlds of film and storytelling. He attended the American Film Institute in 1970 and began shooting *Eraserhead* in 1972; it was a school project that he completed with outside financing. Five years later it was finished, the end product becoming a cult classic. On the strength of *Eraserhead*, Lynch went on to direct *The Elephant Man, Dune,* and then *Blue Velvet*.

Lynch recalled his childhood, according to sources at Paramount Pictures, as "'Good Times on Our Street.' It was 'See Spot Run.' It was beautiful old houses, tree-lined avenues, the milkman, building forts, lots and lots of friends.

It was a dream world, those droning airplanes, blue skies, picket fences, green grass, cherry trees. Middle America the way it was supposed to be. But then on this cherry tree would be this stuff oozing out, some of it black, some of it yellow and there were millions and millions and millions of red ants racing all over the sticky patch, all over the tree. So you see there's this beautiful world and you just look a little bit closer and it's all red ants. There is goodness like those blue skies and flowers and stuff, but there is always a force, a sort of wild pain and decay, accompanying everything."

This paradox influences nearly all of Lynch's work. The same dichotomy—between what is seen and what lurks just below the surface—influenced much of Roberto Rossellini's work. These paradoxes inspire Isabella as well, judging from the controversial, emotionally complex characters she has, so far, chosen to portray.

"I want to do movies that take place in America and that take people into worlds where they could never go," Lynch told L. Borden in "The World According to Lynch," a *Village Voice* article published on September 23, 1986. "Give them a set of images and sounds they couldn't have any other way. Give them journeys into the very depths of their beings. That is really what I'm aiming for!"

The same words could have been spoken by Roberto Rossellini. It is not difficult to understand why their union is still going strong. Isabella and David both bring tremendous passion and love to their relationship.

For Isabella, it is a life that began with her flight from Rome seventeen years earlier.

More and more, Isabella Rossellini is an American. She came to the United States as an unknown and America has been good to her. She has been welcomed and adopted as one of its discoveries. But Isabella has not forgotten her European roots. Isabella, like Ingrid, will probably be an American, as well as an international, star.

Even though Roberto always discouraged Isabella from becoming an actress, and her mother never encouraged her, there is no question that both of her parents would be proud of the path Isabella has not so much chosen as discovered. Although Roberto vehemently disapproved of an acting career for Isabella, he would have been thrilled and impressed by all that she has accomplished. Like any fellow artist, he would have recognized her talent.

Roberto Rossellini caught only a glimpse of his daughter's ascension to international fame before his death in 1977, those glimpses seen in her work as a television journalist. Ingrid saw only the beginning of Isabella's film career before a nine-year struggle with cancer ended with Ingrid's death in 1982. Perhaps she saw in her daughter herself as a young woman—making many of the same mistakes, yet showing flashes of the same brilliance on screen.

Both parents, one would imagine, saw in Isabella traces of themselves and of each other, and more than a little of the legacy of their early love. Were Ingrid and Roberto still alive, they would doubtless look on proudly as their daughter stepped from the shadows of that love.

An early publicity still of Ingrid Bergman just after she left
Sweden under the auspices of David O. Selznick. The
quiet strength of the young actress—already present in
this photo—ultimately led her to international stardom.
© *Neal Peters Collection*

Ingrid—after her long exile—was finally making a comeback by 1955 in the Parisian theatre. Isabella and little Ingrid, both just three years old, and Robertino learned early about the rigors of commuting. Already accustomed to the paparazzi snapping them wherever they went, the children wave good-bye to Ingrid's fans as they leave Rome for Paris.
© *Neal Peters Collection*

Isabella, eleven years old in 1963, stands with her mother and her twin sister in Rome. Ingrid is taking a break from *The Visit*, a movie she made with Anthony Quinn. Already, Isabella's face is taking on the distinct beauty that will help launch her modeling and acting careers almost twenty years later.
© *Pictorial Parade*

Ingrid Bergman and Roberto Rossellini and their three children embody the meaning of family in this snapshot. Pictures, however, can be deceiving, since, in reality, their family life was a far cry from the photograph. The marriage was almost over and a bitter custody battle would soon begin.
© *The Lester Glassner Collection*

Isabella, on the verge of womanhood at the age of fifteen, poses shyly with her favorite dachshund. After Isabella endured a life-threatening operation in which her spine was surgically straightened to prevent a hunchback later in life, she was forced to live inside a cast for almost two years. Her dog, then a puppy, kept her laughing and rarely left her side.
© *Neal Peters Collection*

Ingrid poses with her children, Isabella, Robertino, little Ingrid, and Pia, her only daughter from her marriage to Peter Lindstrom. The picture was taken just after Pia moved to New York to resume her life after spending three years living in Rome, taking care of Ingrid's children by Roberto Rossellini. At the time (1967), Ingrid was appearing at the Broadhurst Theatre in Eugene O'Neill's play *More Stately Mansions*.
© *Neal Peters Collection*

Isabella and her first husband, Martin Scorsese, at a special
screening and party to honor Scorsese's film *New York, New
York*. Their marriage was already under terrible stress, since
Isabella was constantly flying to London to see her mother,
who was struggling with cancer.
© *Ron Galella*

Isabella, a study in quiet, understated European elegance, appears at the screening of her first film, *White Nights*. Her second marriage to Jon Wiedemann broke up during the long shoot, but the seeds were sown for a romance with Mikhail Baryshnikov once they returned to New York.
© *Darlene Hammond/Pictorial Parade*

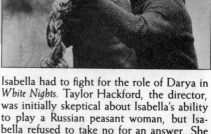

Isabella had to fight for the role of Darya in *White Nights*. Taylor Hackford, the director, was initially skeptical about Isabella's ability to play a Russian peasant woman, but Isabella refused to take no for an answer. She auditioned three times and had to fly to Los Angeles from New York for a screen test before she won the role.
© *Phototeque*

Isabella and Gregory Hines, her costar in *White Nights*, were snapped together at the screening. They became good friends during the shoot, even traveling to Russia together for a long weekend in order to perfect their roles as a long-suffering interracial married couple.
© *Frank Edwards/Fotos International*

Isabella and Robertino, her older brother, have always been close. When Robertino was going through his much publicized breakup with Monaco's Princess Caroline, Isabella helped her brother through the ordeal. When Isabella's brief marriage to Martin Scorsese ended, Robertino helped his sister get over her sense of failure. © *Ron Galella*

Ingrid, Isabella's twin sister, is Isabella's closest confidante. When Ingrid's marriage broke up, she and Tommaso, her son, left Italy and moved to New York City. The two women and their two children, Tommaso and Elettra, lived together in Isabella's Tribeca loft for more than a year, until Ingrid began studying at Columbia and found a place of her own. © *Ron Galella*

Isabella and Pia Lindstrom, her half-sister, share a night out in 1986 at the Museum of Modern Art in New York City for a premiere of Fellini's film *Ginger and Fred*. Pia, a film critic for NBC TV, and Isabella, fresh from *White Nights*, have an enduring friendship, the bonds forged during their time together in Rome when Isabella was a young girl. © *Ron Galella*

Isabella and Renzo Rossellini, her half-brother, attend one of many premieres for Isabella's big-budget Hollywood debut in *White Nights*. Isabella has said many times that she makes no distinction between her half-brothers and -sisters since they all grew up together in Italy like one big happy family, albeit under separate roofs. She is always inviting her European relatives to visit her in New York. © *Ron Galella*

Isabella Rossellini projects mystery and allure in her breakthrough role as Dorothy in David Lynch's *Blue Velvet*. The critics applauded her performance for its depth despite the film's controversial reception. Isabella was determined to make a name for herself her way. While her mother projected an almost archetypal goodness, Isabella so far has embodied many of the darker elements of the human soul in her movie roles.
© *Phototeque*

Isabella looks radiant with David Lynch, her lover for the past three years. Ever since they teamed up together on *Blue Velvet*, the couple has been inseparable. Isabella helped David deal with the jitters in 1988, when he made his big-screen acting debut in *Zelly and Me*, playing her love interest.
© *Steve Granitz/Celebrity Photo*

Isabella is a perfect blend of her Italian father and her Swedish mother. She has the dark Latin coloring of her father, with the high cheekbones and creamy white skin of her mother. It is a face that inspired Lancôme to negotiate a record-breaking $2-million contract in order to convince Isabella to represent their line of cosmetics.
© *Anthony Savignano/Galella Ltd.*

CHAPTER

11

AND THE TIME WAS AT HAND

Sister Pia, a young nun, stared at the contessa. It wouldn't be long now. She felt her wrist. The contessa's skin was pale as parchment; her pulse weak. Her heart was giving out, her spirit undergoing a slow departure from the earthly plane. *How am I to bring comfort to this woman?* the sister wondered. *How is it that Europe's grandest courtesan now lies alone, dying in a charity hospital? Where are her lovers now? Her family?* The contessa's face is lined with age and her beauty has faded, but she is still elegant. She has kept her regal bearing, even as she lies, barely conscious, near death.

The contessa will not die alone, Sister Pia vows, unafraid of death, yet awed by it nonetheless. She adjusts the covers around the old woman; she doesn't want the contessa to be cold.

When Nina arrives, Sister Pia is relieved. Nina is the Contessa's only friend. The contessa deserves to have someone she loves at her bedside—though, strangely, she, Pia, has come to love her as well. She quickly leads Nina to the contessa's bed, then discovers that they are too late.

"I'm sorry," Sister Pia says. "God is with her." She takes a deep breath as Nina absorbs her words. You'd think it would be easier, Pia thinks, remembering all the times she has kept death company, seen life slip away. She did not think she would ever get used to it. No matter how many times she told herself that the dead were now with God, living in God's light, in God's shelter, sadness always followed death. Especially here, where the patients were poor and usually without family or friends.

"Could you tell me," Sister Pia said, "who will take care of the funeral? We or you? If you leave it to us, we'll have to bury her in a common grave."

Nina offers money for the contessa's burial and Sister Pia sees the love Nina has for the contessa. It makes Pia happy to know that the dead woman had at least one person who loved her. Nina asks if the contessa said anything at the end—anything at all.

"She did say something to me at the very end," Sister Pia says, looking up. "'Is life over already?'"

In 1976, Isabella was delivered into the world of film-making by her mother in *A Matter of Time*, when Isabella was twenty-four. Though her mother was an island of calm on the set, Isabella's first cinematic experience as an actress was absolutely horrendous. It was a film that killed friendships, ended or—at least severely hobbled—careers, and left most of the performers without dignity.

"It was a disaster," said Steve Previn, one of the executives in charge of production for the film. "I have gray hair now, but I think every gray hair I got was from that picture. It was almost a full year of total disaster."

The film community was shocked when the picture was released. *A Matter of Time* had been a prestigious picture. Though it had a budget of only $5 million, that was in 1976, when budgets had not yet skyrocketed. All during the shoot, journalists and photographers streamed to Rome to cover the making of the picture. Everyone was intrigued with the elements—Vincente Minnelli as the director; Ingrid Bergman as Europe's most famous courtesan, Charles Boyer as her husband; Liza Minnelli, Tina Aumont, the daughter of actor Jean-Pierre Aumont and the late actress Maria Montez; and Spiros Andros. And, of course, Isabella Rossellini as the sweet-faced nun who tends to the dying contessa, played by her real-life mother. The production was a family affair; Vincente Minelli was working with his daughter for the first time, as was Ingrid Bergman with hers. Isabella's character was even named after her half-sister, Pia Lindstrom.

Isabella never strayed from her mother's side in her small but critically acknowledged first role. It was a satellite role, to be sure, but Isabella made the most of it. In spite of savage reviews, Isabella was singled out for praise. Perhaps unaware of her effect on the film's audience, she created a presence simply by being in the film. And that, as any director will tell you, is the sign of a star: someone in a film whom you feel compelled to watch.

"Isabella inherited this class from her mother," Previn says. "That's the only way to say it. There is nothing starlet about Isabella. She's a lady. Being a lady is something you can't avoid. No matter what she does. Ingrid could play a two-dollar hooker, but she'll always be a lady and Isabella is the same. . . . Isabella has the same innocence as her mother. I think Ingrid told her about makeup. She doesn't add much makeup. She has a very natural look. In the nun outfit she looked lovely. The still photographs were stunning."

"Her father was Rossellini," Previn continued. "What a heritage to overcome. When I met her for the first time at the studio in Rome, I thought that she was just a little daughter of Ingrid's. I hadn't realized that at the time I met her, she was quite well known and on top of the ladder with her own television show. I had no idea. Then I said, 'Gee, she's coming on pretty secure,' and then somebody told me, 'She's more than just a daughter, she's already made a big career for herself.' I lived in Hollywood then and she had a very European-oriented career, though, of course, it isn't anymore."

Isabella had an impressive introduction to the world of Hollywood filmmaking. Though she grew up playing on the sets of her father's films, she had yet to participate in that world. She had not yet learned firsthand the terrible sinking feeling that surrounds a project in which people have lost faith. Once the production goes awry, it can be nearly impossible to rectify the situation. For *A Matter of Time*, it didn't matter that all the elements were bankable or that the cast was star-studded. The film simply wasn't working. At the end of every shooting day, everyone would gather to watch the dailies. At first, everyone was buoyed by the hope that it wasn't that bad. It couldn't be that bad. But it was. Why *A Matter of Time* failed so completely and dismally is something of a mystery, considering John Gay's fine script and the story on which it was based.

A Matter of Time was based on The Film of Memory, a book by Maurice Druon about Marchesa Luisa Casati, one of the most flamboyant personalities of the early 1900s. The story of the contessa, who was played by Ingrid Bergman, is a thinly veiled version of Marchesa Casati's life. With her face painted deathly white, her hair dyed flame red, and her eyes ringed with kohl, the courtesan traveled through Europe, her much-talked-about adventures making her a legend in Venice and Rome.

Marchesa Casati had wax models of her lovers prepared for her viewing pleasure, and was herself painted by the artists Boldini and Augustus John. The marchesa wore gold lamé before the rest of civilization ever heard of it, and was known to arrive at balls wearing a crown of ostrich feathers. Her dresses invariably had trains, and pet cheetahs accompanied her everywhere, restrained by turquoise leashes.

As Liza Minelli told Roderick Mann of the Los Angeles Times in February 8, 1976, "If that isn't a part, I don't know what is!"

The story of Marchesa Casati's life was indeed captivating. The problem was, Liza's father didn't capture it. As a result, there was a lot of fallout from this cinematic bomb.

Steve Previn still remembers Ingrid Bergman's reaction to the finished picture. "One thing that this picture did which I will regret forever was that I lost my friendship with Ingrid Bergman. She was a marvelous, marvelous lady. She trusted me through all the problems on this picture. She trusted that somehow, it would turn out okay, that no one would lose their dignity. When the picture was all finished, she wrote me a very nasty letter saying, 'My God, I thought I could trust you.' It was terrible, just terrible. I was ready for the letter, though, because the picture was such an ordeal."

It is not surprising Isabella grew to have a great deal of ambivalence about the movie business. This was her first taste of the behind-the-scenes battles indigenous to all film projects, but particularly brutal in Hollywood, where most directors view their movies as their children.

Vincente Minelli was no exception. The award-winning director was unhappy about the way the American producer edited his picture. Usually, directors edit their own pictures; producers step in only when they fear the picture isn't "working" and feel they need to "save" it. What usually happens in these situations is disastrous—both director and producer end up making excuses for the movie.

When *A Matter of Time* premiered, the reviews were scathing at worst, condescending at best. Even so, Ingrid Bergman is powerful in this, one of her last roles. There is a particular poignancy when Ingrid, as the contessa, realizes she is seventy-two and will never be young again, never enjoy the flattery of young men. Ingrid always drew from her own life for her roles and we sense her own pain at growing old when the camera moves in for a close-up.

"I was terribly worried that *A Matter of Time* was going to be her swan song and it had no right to be," Previn says. "Thank God she did one more picture after that with Ingmar Bergman. She plays the mother and Liv Ullman plays the daughter in *Autumn Sonata*. A great movie. That's the one she went out with and not this piece of garbage."

Ingrid Bergman's last role was that of the former Israeli prime minister, Golda Meir. Many considered this to be Ingrid's most brilliant portrayal. As Ingrid's time in the spotlight was coming to an end, Isabella's time had come.

It is interesting that both Isabella and Liza had a famous actress for a mother and a famous director for a father and both had to struggle to find their place in the world. When they worked together on *A Matter of Time*, Liza had just come into her own with the release of *Cabaret* and Isabella was naturally in awe of her. On the up side, however, Isabella was able to test the waters as an actress with some amount of support. Liza Minnelli is known as a generous and playful actress, always good to her fellow actors. Her father, too, created a wonderful atmosphere on the set of *A Matter of Time*, in spite of all the worry that the picture wasn't holding up. His artists were protected as much as possible from distractions and treated to the best of everything. The hoopla that attends the production of a prestigious picture was impressive to the young and inexperienced Isabella.

Both Liza and Ingrid worked hard to keep everyone's spirits up during the difficult shoot, with different results. "Ingrid Bergman, was one of the all time great ladies," Previn says. "Lady, not movie star. She kept everything going.

"We had a crew of about sixty people and every single week, Ingrid would go to one of the crew members and ask, 'Are you married? Do you have children?' She'd find out and then she'd say, 'Why don't you get a babysitter for your kids and you and your wife come have dinner with me and you tell me where your favorite bistro is.' Every single week, two or three times a week, she'd go out with a different crew member, the result being that at the end of the picture, people would have cut off their right arm for Ingrid Bergman.

"When Christmas came, it was Ingrid who got all the

hand-knit sweaters. It was touching. She was a marvelous lady."

Isabella has the same sense of class as her mother. She also inherited her serene cinematic presence. The first-time actress was singled out by Pauline Kael, the *New Yorker* film critic, in an unusual accolade for a first role: "Isabella Rossellini appears here in the small role of a nun and is a soft, ethereal version of Bergman in *The Bells of St. Mary's*, but with an Italian accent. It must be a relief to Bergman to pass her nun's habit on to her daughter and bask in the contessa's fancy duds and Circean melancholy."

"She really was quite good," adds Previn. "She was in a nun's uniform and she did very well, very well. At the time she was not really an actress, but she handled it very well. She brought a real innocence to the role without her mother coaching. Ingrid just kept her going. She didn't coach her."

Characteristically, Isabella shrugs off the importance of her film debut. "It was sort of fun because the scene was so short," she said to Lawrence Eisenberg in a February 1983 *Cosmopolitan* article. Her passion for acting still lay dormant.

"Right now," she told Eisenberg in 1983, "I don't have an ultimate goal. I'm too confused. I have a goal for maybe a year. Some people know when they are children what they want to be as grownups. I always thought I was going to be a veterinarian or a trainer of lions for the circus. My dream now, I know it's an unusual one, would be to work on an educational program for the BBC."

That dream faded, as dreams sometimes do. Isabella did not go on to work for the BBC. Instead, she became a respected actress in her own right, choosing controversial roles in controversial movies, surprising some, like Steve Previn, by her choices.

Perhaps his biggest surprise was *Blue Velvet*.

"I was ashamed for her," says Previn. "I knew her mother quite well. And I wish she hadn't done that. I think if her mother had been alive, she wouldn't have."

But her mother did die; her life, like the Contessa's, came to an end just as Isabella's life was beginning. As she began to step from the shadows, Isabella started embracing her own choices. Her first major film role was about a young woman forced to make difficult choices, because by choosing she could grow and embrace life. In this case, art imitated life.

CHAPTER
12

IF IT PLEASES YOU, DO IT

Eugenia glances at Giovanni. He looks like a young boy with the sun shining down on his sweet face in this place, their secret meadow. She loves him, but how can she? Her life, her dreams, are with Enzo. How can she love both men passionately? And they both love her. She sees it in the way they look at her, the way they laugh at her jokes, the way they turn toward her when she speaks their names. With them, she feels strong, strong enough to work toward her dream. All her life, her dreams have soared like angels in her mind, but the older one gets, she has discovered, the harder it is to make those angels come to earth. Her dreams are quite simple, really. She wants to bring laughter and love to the countryside with the children's theater. And live on the farm with Enzo. They've planned their future together.

Giovanni can't fit into their dreams, she knows, and yet he fits into her heart as though he were always there. She looks at Enzo. She looks at Giovanni. She won't think about it. She will simply drink this day in the meadow into her very soul. She wants to remember this time, this time of youth and dreams.

In the 1979 Italian film *Il Prato* (*The Meadow*), Isabella played the role of Eugenia as a tribute to her father. Roberto Rossellini's spirit was on the set of *The Meadow* every day, so much so that the still-inexperienced actress had trouble concentrating during the shooting of certain scenes.

"I wanted to do the film for its reference to my father and because it was an opportunity to spend time with Paolo and Vittorio, the Taviani brothers," Isabella told Joseph Gelmis in a May 23, 1982 *Los Angeles Times* article. She was referring to the fact that footage from one of her father's films, *Germany Year Zero*, is featured in *The Meadow*.

"For them, Father was a maestro. Their link with my father's last fight was very important to me. In a romantic and sentimental way, I transferred my feelings for him to them. That became painful during the love scenes. I've always been very afraid of acting. Father didn't want us to act. He was very jealous of sharing his children with strangers. The hardest scene for me in *The Meadow* was kissing the other actor in front of Paolo and Vittorio. In a way, they were representing my father."

The Taviani brothers led her into the world of acting with a father's love. Her transference was well placed, since both brothers have carried on the legacy of Roberto Rossellini. Paolo and Vittorio clearly hold Isabella's father in the highest regard, and have continued his approach to filmmaking.

Like Rossellini, the brothers believe in telling a story, not dominating the screen with technique and fancy camera moves. They believe the art of film lies in capturing a simple reality, not creating a false one.

"We do not have a theory, about this, you understand, but from the beginning we have sought simplicity," Paolo Taviani told John Powers in the July 24, 1987 edition of the *L.A. Weekly*. "We have never been interested in those big swoops of the camera, even though magnificent movies have been made that way. It's been our vocation to try not to bluff, to try not to overplay with the camera, but to let the characters live in their landscape while we look at them in the simplest way." By giving her heart to the role of Eugenia, Isabella was inspired to do a bit of emotional housekeeping before she could really commit herself to the acting profession.

"I would first have to overcome guilt," she said. "Because my father would feel so bad if I became an actress."

It is difficult to believe that Roberto Rossellini, the consummate artist, could have objected to Isabella's first starring vehicle. But parental disapproval is a strong force for an adult child to overcome.

If Isabella made a movie her mother's way the first time out—*A Matter of Time* was a splashy Hollywood production, its commercial failure notwithstanding—then her second film was closer to one of her father's. *The Meadow* was a low-budget film that explored the spiritual issues of existence. Ironically, it was her father's death that led her to the role of Eugenia.

Roberto headed the 1977 Cannes Film Festival jury that

awarded the prestigious Golden Palm award to *Padre Padrone*, a film the Taviani brothers made just before *The Meadow*.

"I was keeping my father company in Cannes," Isabella told William Wolf in "Heiress to Greatness," an August 1982 article that appeared in *New York* magazine. "He loved *Padre Padrone* and was very proud that a film made in 16mm for television had won at such an important festival.

"It was a victory for my father's ideas about what films should be. He was very involved in social problems and very much for low-budget cinema and reaching the largest number of people through television."

Because of his love for *Padre Padrone*, Rossellini fought hard for it to win top honors. His efforts paid off. It cost a hundred thousand dollars, was made for television, and it won against the big 35mm films coming from America and Europe.

Isabella and Roberto spent a lot of time with Paolo and Vittorio Taviani during the film festival that year. They hated to see it end since they had shared such a moment of exaltation when *Padre Padrone* won the most prestigious awards. It was the last time the Taviani brothers would see their former mentor alive. A few weeks after the festival ended, Roberto Rossellini died suddenly.

"I became very close to the Tavianis," Isabella told William Wolf. "They came to the funeral in Rome. They were really so much in love with my father and inspired by him. When they asked me to be in *The Meadow*, it would have been really hard to say no." Especially, one might add, considering that the film pays a wonderful homage to Rossellini. In *The Meadow* Isabella's character watches part of her father's 1947 film *Germany Year Zero*. It's a film within a film. Isabella was concerned that such a scene might seem ridiculous, but, in the end, she was pleased with the results.

"It worked out fine," she said. "Nobody in Italy complained about that or found it campy."

It is no surprise that Isabella was drawn to the same kind of material her father found so fascinating during his long career. And there was a certain poetry, a certain rightness, to the idea of working with two filmmakers who had been inspired by her father's work.

Like Roberto Rossellini, the Taviani brothers always made films their way. They were convinced that the only way to achieve a universal response was to "be faithful to what you know best and what you care about most," as Vittorio Taviani told John Powers in the July 24, 1987 *L.A. Weekly*.

Rossellini's ideology is carried on by his former students—and by his daughter. And just as the Taviani brothers looked up to Rossellini as young filmmakers, so Isabella looked up to the Taviani brothers.

Even though Isabella was making a low-budget, somewhat esoteric picture, she did not escape the media attention that comes with being the daughter of world-famous parents. During the first few days of shooting, flashbulbs exploded endlessly and photographers cataloged her every move on the set.

"*The Meadow* was made in a village, and the people gathered to stare at me," Isabella told William Wolf. "The paparazzi came too. I was very intimidated."

Isabella's fear, however, does not show up in a single frame. Like her mother, she refused to let distractions interfere with her work. Perhaps having her family nearby helped. Isabella's in-laws at the time, Charles and Catherine Scorcese, portray train passengers in one scene.

There is no doubt that Isabella is an unpolished actress in *The Meadow*. But it was, after all, her first real starring role. Her radiance and natural openness, however, carry her a long way. By watching all her mother's films, she learned a great deal about the "less is more" school of acting.

"I'm enchanted," Isabella once said, referring to her mother. "Naturally, as a daughter, but also as a model, by her way of talking and moving. She has incredible charm; she is so simple, so direct, so down to earth."

While rehearsing for the film, Isabella recalled in a *New York Times* article of June 18, 1982, the advice her mother once gave her: "'Just keep it simple. Don't do anything.' And I said, 'If I don't do anything, I will look like a piece of log.' But she was right. I don't have the skills to embellish, so I kept it simple, and I'm sort of proud. I think I did a good job. I wasn't pretentious. But it wasn't great acting, either."

Isabella has learned the valuable maxim "be smart enough to know what you don't know." "My performance was very simple," she told John Skow of *Time* magazine. "But it was correct. At least I don't make a gesture or deliver a line that's out of place. When you're an amateur, the danger is that you exaggerate. Mother gave me a very good point of view. 'If you don't know how to do something, don't do anything' she said. 'If the scene is sad and you're looking ironical, you create a misunderstanding.' So every time I was in trouble, I just made a blank face and hoped the violins and the light hitting my face would take care of it.

"You know, though, sometimes it's good to be afraid. When I was on live television, it was very frightening, but I used the fear and the shyness, because I thought there was some sort of humanity and charm in being completely real. But it has to be a little bit in control, because if you have no control, you're not a pro."

As Isabella told Joseph Gelmis in the May 23, 1982 *Los Angeles Times* article, "A Child of the Movies Makes Movies," "Mother is able to draw feelings on her face. I don't have those skills. I don't know if I have the talent to do it someday. When I called mother I wanted to know if she thought I could do the movie, if I should do it, since I was afraid there would be some expectations because I am her daughter. Mother said, 'If it pleases you, do it.'"

After the rigorous shoot, Isabella's confidence as an actress grew. She told William Wolf, "I can do anything," she said. "Have any kind of career I want."

Still, the truth of her words didn't really sink in until later. It was only after both her parents died that Isabella really took up the acting gauntlet. She had always been reluctant to tread on their turf, partly from respect, partly from fear, partly from indecision. Yet when her mother died, Isabella found herself free of the past and able to make the choices she had always hesitated about.

"By then, the way of being respectful by not acting on longer seemed the only way," Isabella told Charles Champlin in a November 14, 1985 *Los Angeles Times* article. "I'd done film as a sort of amateur, but now I had to be responsible; I couldn't use film as a school. I wanted to see for myself if I liked acting, and if I had any ability."

Isabella discovered she had more than ability. She had inspiration. And no one was more surprised than she was.

"All of a sudden it seemed to be fun and passionate and interesting."

CHAPTER

13

CLICK!
THE CAMERA LOVES YOU!

sabella stretches langorously, like a cat waking up from a nap. She can hear the crew outside her trailer, preparing for the next shot. She breathes deeply. The air in Puerto Rico is different from the air in New York. It has a crisp, clean smell as it blows in from the ocean.

Time to get back to work. Stepping from her trailer, Isabella squints at the sun, high and hot overhead. The art director smiles at her. Isabella smiles back. She touches her big belly. She's six months pregnant and the baby is also waking up from their nap, stretching and poking. She rubs her stomach, trying to quiet her child. Her tactic works.

When the lights are in place and the camera is positioned, the assistant director indicates that the setup is ready. The director looks for his star. Their eyes meet. Before Isabella can say a word, the makeup woman takes her in hand, powders her nose, touching up her face with satiny brushes. It is not difficult to bring out Isabella's beauty. Her wide cheekbones are accented with peach blush; her lips— full and sensuous—need only a bit of color. She epitomizes feminine elegance.

Isabella's eyes glance around the set as the makeup woman does her magic. The deserted road does, in fact, look like France. The palm trees are carefully cropped out of the shot. The Lancôme executives, oddly out of place in their pin-stripe business suits, seem pleased.

"Quiet on the set," yells the second assistant director. The director speaks softly to Isabella. He explains that she is a woman without a lover, enjoying the sensuous beauty of the glorious French countryside. Isabella listens intently, then nods. She's ready. The director watches as Isabella becomes the woman he's described, a serene woman in love with all of creation.

Isabella rides her bicycle down the lonely country road, her basket filled with wildflowers. She rides alone, daydreaming under the azure sky. The camera tracks her, staying close on her face in order to keep her big belly out of view. She glides around a bend. A shy smile lights her face when she sees a herd of cows blocking her path.

The cowherd, French to the core with his black beret and smock, shoos the cows away to clear her path. He finds her lovely. She offers him a flower from her basket and his eyes twinkle with pleasure.

The director reshoots the scene again and again. He covers her short ride with as many angles as possible so that he will have lots of footage from which to choose once he's in the editing room. Isabella pedals away, never seeming to tire. Between takes, she rests, glowing with health and vitality. She looks like a woman born to be a mother. Each time the camera rolls, Isabella brings something new to the scene, *some added bit of mystery, or a new look in her eye. It's one of the actor's hardest jobs, keeping it fresh.*

Thirty-five people watch, the crew, the advertising team, the bigwigs from Lancôme. Isabella grabs, then holds, their confidence as she breezes through the day, always prepared, always ready when the director needs her. Just before the camera rolls, she steadies herself, concentrating completely on the task at hand.

A totally professional actress—as was her mother.

Between takes, when the lighting director struggles to control the lighting "hot spots" that occur when the sun streaks in and out of the clouds, Isabella dispels the tension from the delay with her boisterous laughter and her high spirits.

———

Frances Grill changed Isabella's life. She singlehandedly launched Isabella's record-breaking modeling career. This gray-haired New Yorker, nearing sixty, enjoys her full powers as a woman at an age when many have retired to the suburbs for the quiet life. She cracked the tough nut of the glitzy New York modeling world by creating a small, renegade modeling agency named Click and naming herself president. This minuscule, unorthodox company had an inauspicious start in 1980. Grill raised her initial start-up capital by mortgaging her house in Queens for thirty thousand dollars. Her money could not have been better spent. Frances—and, by extension, Click—became known for unusual models with unusual attributes.

"I'd look at the magazines and realize that nobody I knew looked that way, though I knew a lot of beautiful people," Grill explained to Brad Gooch in "Will Flick Click?" a November 1987 article in *Vanity Fair.* "When choosing a model, you don't look for the pretty face at all.

I look for form—strong jawline, the spread of the eyes, the voluptuousness of a mouth. It's really a subjective thing, though."

The subjective strategy of Frances Grill was brilliant—or perhaps it was the age-old story of having the right idea at the right time. Regardless, Click is currently grossing some $16 million in billing and boasts a stable of two hundred models.

Chance brought Isabella and Frances together. While still married to Ulf Lundqvist, a Swedish menswear designer, Frances hosted a Swedish midsummer night's party. Isabella, a friend of a friend, was a guest. The two women hit it off immediately.

At the time, Isabella was an Italian celebrity—not only because of her famous parents, but because of her David Letterman—style interviews for Italian television.

The daughter of a Brooklyn longshoreman, Frances was a wife and mother before she became an astute businesswoman. After her second marriage with Lundqvist ended, Frances took up with the New York avant-garde and found herself inspired by the work of the trend-setting European photographers. Relying on instinct, Frances convinced some of these new photographers to let her represent them in the American market. Suddenly, Frances was in business representing unknown talent in highly competitive New York.

It was not an easy task, but one Frances tackled with vigor. After aggressively making her name as a photographer's agent, Frances branched out. And Click was born.

"I named it Click in honor of the camera, which had been my livelihood for so many years," explained Frances, a dynamo who was literally blind to the competition. At the time, the four major modeling agencies—Ford, Wilhemina, Elite, and Zoli—always grabbed the big accounts.

Rejecting the blonde, blue-eyed Ford Agency–type model, Frances sent out exotic, ethnic models, the same models bigger agencies had rejected because of their "unmarketable" looks.

Enter Isabella. After their initial meeting in Europe, chance once again brought the two women together, when Isabella began dating a photographer Frances happened to represent.

"When I opened Click, Isabella asked what could she do to help me get the agency off the ground," recalled Frances to Brad Gooch. "Become a model," I said.

"There is a timelessness about Isabella that conflicts with the trendiness of the fashion business," Frances told Gooch. "She has a freshness about her. We got into a cab once and the driver told her, 'You sound like a wonderful actress who used to live in America—her name was Ingrid Bergman.' Isabella turned red as a beet and when I told him that Bergman was her mother, he refused to believe me. Her background makes her unique."

Isabella's entry into the world of modeling was also unique. On any given day in Manhattan, hundreds of would-be models make the rounds. They traverse the island on endless "go-sees," hoping their face will impress someone with the power to hire them. Isabella joined their ranks.

Helen Murray, a photographer's agent who was working with Calvin Klein at the time, was not impressed with Isabella when she first met her.

"To me it was an Italian movie star go-see, so I thought,

great!" Helen recalled to Brad Gooch. "But when I picked her up in reception, I couldn't believe it. She had no makeup on. She was dressed in what one would sort of call frumpy clothes. I thought, she wants to be a model? I'm the first to admit, I didn't get it."

Frances had a problem: To make a success of Isabella and properly launch her modeling career, she needed Isabella to be available for more appointments. Her future star client was still putting in long hours on her Italian television show. Acting again on instinct, Frances asked Isabella to leave her show for ten months. Frances promised to find her a contract in that period of time.

Frances knew what she was doing. Moving quickly, she lined up the best photographers in the business to prepare a stunning portfolio for Isabella. Her test shots turned out better than Frances could have dreamed. No one can explain why a camera takes to a face. The darkroom is the only place one finds out for sure if the chemistry between the model and camera is successful.

"Frances asked me to pose for some photographers," Isabella told Brad Gooch. "So I said, 'If you want me to, I'd love to.'

"So I worked with Bruce Weber and Bill King and right away I got the cover of *Vogue*. It was very unexpected. I thought it was wonderful to be able to work for a day or two with these great photographers and to have these wonderful pictures of myself. I thought I was going to buy a lot of copies of the magazine and show them later on to my grandchildren and say, 'Look how pretty I was when I was young.' I didn't really think it was going to be a major career. I don't think anybody else thought so either."

Frances disagrees. She did think so. And she was a

woman of her word. Within a few months, she snared a $2 million contract for Isabella with Lancôme.

The newly discovered model felt she was part of a family at Click—an eccentric family, but a family nonetheless.

"They're very loose," Isabella told Gooch. "You don't have to be just a model or an actress. You can paint. There are so many people they represent in the agency—a magician, a transvestite. I always thought that was fun. It's like a circus."

The difference, of course, is that Frances's circus made her a millionaire. It is no mystery why Lancôme shelled out a record $2 million for a relative unknown with little camera experience. Not only did Isabella have an impeccable lineage, but she was also a stunning and classic beauty. It's more of a mystery why Isabella, after ten years as a television journalist, celebrity interviewer, and occasional actress, decided to become a model.

It was not a planned career change, that's for sure. "Here I pose once," Isabella said to Gooch, wonderment in her words, "And I am on *Vogue*. It's a miracle."

One thing was certain—the camera loved Isabella Rossellini as much as it had her mother.

"She's not the commercial face that we've been used to in the seventies," recalled Polly Mellen, to Gooch, fashion editor at *Vogue*. "It's very exciting, personally, to realize another kind of look is coming forward. Isabella gives back a picture of a vulnerable, real, intelligent human being with the quality of being a comedian at the same time. I find her a very beautiful person—inside and out."

Isabella's new career was not met with approval by everyone. Social by nature, Isabella has always valued the opinions of her friends. It comes from growing up in Italy, where everyone has an opinion, and impassioned arguments are as common as chit-chat. Her Italian friends did not applaud her entry into the world of American marketing and capitalism as the Lancôme girl. They thought she was selling out.

With the ease of a seasoned politician, Isabella took it all in stride. "I had all that moralistic attitude, too," Isabella says with a shrug. "It was very much a thing of the early seventies . . . but I think some of my friends would be less severe on me now.

"They say that people who succeed are surrounded by envy, and that's true, but some of it is the moral argument: Should you be a model, should women be represented like that? I don't have an answer. I sort of like being in doubt."

Like her father, she always seeks the deeper issues, never accepting the easy way out, always questioning.

"Women in advertisements are represented as very beautiful and very rich, wearing fancy clothes and makeup and all that, and not everybody can afford those things. So sometimes, instead of creating a fantasy, you create a complex in some women who know there's no way they can get near that point.

"It's very hard to answer the question of whether as a model you are portraying a sort of ideologically bad image of women. I had some initial feelings about that and I still have them. But I feel proud of my work as a model. I'm happy that when people in the industry talk about my work as a model they always say that my beauty is different. For example I am not sixteen—I started when I was twenty-eight . . . . and I don't have blue eyes, I'm not blond, I don't have a cute, available smile."

Bruce Weber expressed it best when he told Brad

Gooch: "Isabella has turned everything around, making age, depth, experience, and substance attractive."

Despite her moral qualms, Isabella became a top model almost overnight. She appeared on the covers of *Vogue*, *Harper's Bazaar*, *Vanity Fair*, and *Elle*. All the best photographers wanted to take her picture: Richard Avedon, Bruce Weber, Norman Parkinson, and Eve Arnold. When she signed her contract with Lancôme, her face became known worldwide in a campaign that has, so far, been presented in a hundred and forty countries, on television and in print.

All over the world, millions of people saw the same thing: a serene, self-possessed aura; a face reminiscent, yet independent of her famous mother; luminous doe eyes that seem, paradoxically, womanly and childlike at the same instant.

She makes it look easier than it is. "I think all models feel insecure," Isabella admits to Alexandra Witchel in a January 1986 *Elle* magazine article, with her customary honesty and forthrightness. "Each one of them has a fixation about one part of her body or another." Isabella pauses, remembering the operation that left her scarred for life. "I did feel—well, deformed is a very heavy word, but maybe just a little deformed. Becoming a model, though, has reinforced the feeling that I'm all right!"

The serene face that millions of women admire every day does not bely Isabella's ambition and passion for a job well done. Work inspires her. She has, she says, a "passion for the things I love."

"I love the photographers and I guess they like me," Isabella told *Life* magazine in November 1985, pleasure evident in her voice. "I am disciplined, very punctual, and I can drop three pounds fast if they ask. I'm just an angel!"

Isabella laughs, exposing the one flaw in her features: a chipped front tooth. Somehow, it makes her even more attractive; she didn't try to hide it, or fix it, or cap it. Her beauty just happens to be a part of her. It is not a separate entity to be worked on and manipulated.

"I think teeth have their own equilibrium . . ." she says, trailing off, not sure if she's chosen the right word for James Brady in an October 5, 1986 *Parade* magazine article. Being fluent in several languages can be confusing. "I have perfect teeth, no cavities, just this big chip. My brother broke it when he threw a telephone at me. He would insult my girlfriends with obscenities on the phone. I once tried to take it away and he let go. I have to laugh. If I let them start changing my teeth, then they will change something else, and then I will not be me."

Isabella would be unwilling to give up this prize she worked so hard to win: herself.

"I wish I had started things sooner, so they would last longer," Isabella said in the November 1985 issue of *Life* magazine, her words laced with a touch of melancholy. "I like all this so much—being a model, being an actress now. But maybe if I had done it all earlier, I wouldn't have enjoyed it because I couldn't have appreciated it to the full extent. I wasn't a grown-up woman."

Isabella was clearly a late bloomer. Before she found her way, she was still a child trying to find her own way in a dark world.

CHAPTER

14

WITH LUCK,
YOU FIND A VOICE

Darya stares in mute horror as her husband degrades himself yet again. Her heart aches. She feels powerless to stop the slow burn of his pain, the pain of a vanquished career.

Their love was spawned in such a glory of light. Raymond, a child of the ghetto, fled the country that offered him no shelter and no future for a place where he prayed life would hold more promise. He was a tap dancer, Harlem born, bred, and trained. Russia was his great hope. But that was years ago; his hope was almost dead now, slowly strangled by a system that had once welcomed but soon forgot him.

Siberia was their home. Together, they brought a little magic to the barren land with its deprived, lonely people. They hoped one day to *make enough money to move back to Moscow. Maybe Nikolai could help somehow, Darya thinks as she turns away from her husband, drunk on vodka, tapping his heart out in a staccato rhythm. Nikolai Rodchenko. A dancer. A great dancer. Why had Colonel Chaiko brought this man to live with them? And why was Raymond so willing to help the colonel, a man who had used them, then discarded them like unwanted children.*

Tap. Tap. Tap.

Darya watched her husband move across the wooden floor in their shabby apartment and it happened again. When he danced, he was magic. She felt his pain when he danced; she felt his very essence. She looked at him with love, marveling at all the ways a woman can love a man. She loved him like a mother, wanting only the best for him. She loved him like a sister, wanting to tease the laughter from him. And she loved him like a lover, wanting him all to herself. Finally, he stopped dancing. Her heart burned, knowing what it cost him to dance at home, with no audience, no lights, no applause. He collapsed next to her and she held him close, covering his face with kisses, stroking his beautiful dark skin with her hands. She would never stop trying to take away his pain.

Taylor Hackford's *White Nights* was inspired by Mikhail Baryshnikov, who thought of the idea for the film after discussing a recurring nightmare with James Goldman, a screenwriter. Baryshnikov, a Russian defector, frequently dreamed that he was forced to move back to Russia years after his defection and it was not a pleasant reunion. Working from that initial concept, Goldman wrote the script.

Taylor Hackford, the director of *An Officer and a Gentleman* and *Against All Odds*, was the first American director to cast Isabella Rossellini in a major role in a big-budget film.

"As a director, Taylor felt that he had a great talent in Isabella and it would be nice to break that talent." said Bill Borden, the associate producer of *White Nights*.

Hackford almost lost Isabella. Peter Yates wanted to cast her opposite Harrison Ford in *Witness* after she'd been cast as Darya in *White Nights*.

"You can't blame Taylor for saying, 'Hey, I found her and I'd like to be the first one to have her out in a movie,'" Borden continued. "There is some publicity to be gleaned from being the first to use an actress of that caliber. Every director should, inherently, be selfish. Isabella was asked to do *Witness* in between the time that we cast her and the time we needed her. We cast three or four months in advance. I think she needed an extra week or two. We couldn't move our start dates, which would have made it possible for her to do the other picture. There was nothing hostile at all. We did our picture and we were sorry she couldn't do anything in between our casting her and the other picture but the dates just didn't work out for us.

"To move a picture off a week or two costs money and the financial reality is that you'd spend thousands of dollars because an actress wants to do another picture. It's bad business. It comes down to financially it's not a smart business decision. Also, they might say 'We need her for five weeks,' but what if their picture goes over schedule? Then what do you do? You're really in trouble at that point because an actor is contractually bound to the job until he finishes it."

Hackford got his way.

More than in any of her other films, Isabella evokes her

mother's image in *White Nights*. It's in her face, even her gestures. Her accent differs, but the voice is the same. And, in one sense, Isabella owes her screen debut in *White Nights* to another family member—Elettra, her daughter. For when Isabella became pregnant, she grew fat.

"And fat models don't work," she told Bruce Cook in a November 28, 1985 *Chicago Tribune* article. "So I had time to at last go to acting school in New York. I worked with Sandra Seacat. I was really glad I worked with her. I still do. Through her, I got an agent. Through the agent, I got an appointment to see Taylor for the part in *White Nights*."

Though it sounds easy, it wasn't. Hollywood hype promotes the idea people are still "discovered" sitting at the soda counter in Schwab's drug store. The problem is, Schwab's has been gone for years.

In reality, Taylor Hackford was unsure about casting someone so inexperienced in such a major role. Isabella wasn't Russian and she couldn't even do a Russian accent. Yet something made him open to being convinced. The critically acclaimed director told her that if she worked on her accent, she could come and audition for him again.

Wasting no time, Isabella immediately started studying Russian. By the time she had a second meeting with Taylor, her accent was much improved. The next meeting was even more important. She was to meet Mikhail Baryshnikov and Gregory Hines. By the time this meeting occurred, Isabella was in great form.

Their meeting went well, Isabella could feel it. But she knew Taylor was still not convinced the elements—the three stars—were right. Two weeks after their second meeting, he flew Isabella out to Los Angeles for a screen test.

"Taylor tends to read and screen-test actors as much as possible," Borden says. "He'll do it as much as the actors let him. Even someone of Isabella's caliber, and even though she's a great actress, she was untried and it's best to test someone as a director and let the studio—the guys who are investing a tremendous amount of money—see some footage.

"You don't say to an actress, 'The reason we're testing you is to see if you can act.' The reason we test actresses is to see if they're right for the role with the elements.

"Even Helen Mirren [a well-known, much-respected English actress] tested for the part. There is no question that Helen Mirren can act. The question is, how will she look in this role, how will she handle it? At the time, Helen was not a known commodity in Hollywood. Even though she was a famous actress in Europe, the studio didn't know what they were getting so the best thing was to [have her] read with the director three or four times and do a screen test. Isabella went through the same process."

Finally, Isabella was offered the part. Suddenly, she had her first major role. She was a working actress. In a whirlwind of excitement, she set off for the various European locations.

"We shot all over Scotland, Finland, England, and Portugal," Borden says. "All the footage from Russian streets was shot in Russia. That's a very difficult thing to do. I went to Russia four times to do scouting. We ended up buying footage from a company in Leningrad to put in our film.

"We sent Isabella to Russia," Borden adds. "She went for five days with Gregory Hines. We sent them over there to hang out in Russia and we introduced them to some people and they partied and walked around Leningrad."

Isabella can't say enough nice things about her co-stars. She told Bruce Cook in a November 28, 1985 *Chicago Tribune* article, "Gregory is a fantastic guy. I was lucky to have both him and Misha to work with. They were so helpful and protective, wonderful men and wonderful dancers.

"We worked six months together. And when it was all over, I missed them so much. The only sad thing about working in films is that you get to feel so close to people, and when it's over, you miss them so much."

Isabella didn't have to miss Misha for very long. "We are best friends, and I know he has that woman reputation thing," Isabella said in *Life*. "For our love affair, we sublimate—is that the word?—with our dogs. His female dachshund just had six puppies by mine. Just say the dogs had the affair and Misha and I skipped the trouble.

"I really liked it, being on the set and acting—though I didn't really know how—I just obeyed. I listened very carefully and I thought, 'When I know more, then I'll offer things.'"

Isabella clearly loved the experience and the movie. She saw two screenings before the film was released to the public.

"The first time I was overwhelmed by the dance," Isabella told Bruce Cook, "I knew they were doing wonderful things. I always watched their rehearsals and every time they shot. Taylor moved the camera a lot during the dance sequences and I knew some very interesting things were being done.

"Then the second time I saw it, I thought, 'What a wonderful suspense—very entertaining, you know. It's a very rich film, so many elements to it. I was very happy to be involved with a big film like this. We even exploded an airplane! And now it will open, and I am very happy for that because now I get to see Gregory and Misha again."

Borden has no doubt that Isabella contributed to the

performance of her co-stars. "Isabella was a tremendous moral support to Misha and Gregory," he says. "There was no prima donna behavior by anyone. Everyone pitched in to make the best movie we could."

Their efforts paid off. Isabella was received with open arms by the public. Though she played a plain, even frumpy housewife, at certain angles it was impossible not to see her mother's legacy in the beauty of her face. The daughter of a screen legend had now undeniably found her metier: acting.

"People always told me I should try to be an actress because of my mother, but that's not a very good reason," Isabella told *Screen Test* magazine in November 1985.

As Taylor Hackford told the same interviewer, Isabella first caught his eye when he saw her picture in a magazine layout, in which she looked "so versatile, so virginal in one pose, so pink in another, yet like her famous mother in still another."

The director found a magic in Isabella—the person as well as the actress. One night in particular stands out in his mind. When the cast and crew were on location in Pori, Finland, Isabella celebrated her mother's birthday on the second anniversary of her death.

"Isabella had each of us sing a song," Hackford says. "She simply wanted to transmit the joy in her love for her mother to all of us on the film. And she did. When we finally left the restaurant that cold night, we had such genuine feelings. It was impossible to be immune to Isabella's great spirit and friendship."

Bill Borden recounts another magical night, in a small Italian restaurant in London. "Isabella planned the entire evening," Borden says. "There were about ten of us—including Gregory, Misha, Taylor, myself, Jerzy Skolimowski, Helen

Mirren, Robert Duvall, and Christopher Walken. We all wore costumes, different hats and things. We were definitely odd men out in this fancy little restaurant.

"The owners knew Isabella and she was the star, more than anyone else. We had a big sit-down dinner. And at one point in the evening, everyone did a crazy little thing.

"Isabella and Helen did a fake striptease. They had other clothes on underneath. It was absolutely hilarious. They brought in this guy who did Swiss yodeling while he played the accordion. When Taylor left that night, he was wearing a Viking helmet when he got into his taxi."

It all sounds suspiciously like Isabella's father, a man of great imagination and playfulness who came to life at a party.

To hear others speak of Isabella, it seems as if she lives a charmed life. Isabella hotly contests that notion.

"Sometimes people assume that if you are Ingrid Bergman's daughter—or Roberto Rossellini's daughter—that's it! You don't have anything to worry about," Isabella told Alice Steinbach in "On Her Own," a November 1985 article published in the *Saturday Review*. "I don't think that's true. But I can't deny it does help at the beginning. I mean, casting directors, agents, producers, they're kind of willing to meet me, and that's hard for most actors—to get the appointment. It's easier for me. But then you have to do the rest yourself. You have to work at it."

Isabella remembers how hard she had to work to play Darya. "I learned English in Sweden," she says. "My mother taught me. When I first met Taylor, he had some reservations, I guess because I wasn't Russian. At first, there was a wall between us. There was this feeling I got from him. 'Lovely meeting you, maybe another film, another time.' But then we talked and we had a drink and after that he seemed more flexible, more interested. I said, 'Let me try. Let me work on my accent and study some Russian.' So he said yes. But he didn't promise anything."

Once shooting began, everyone was thrilled with Isabella's professional, capable demeanor. Her actions were not those of a novice.

"Isabella was very brave when we shot the scene where she and Misha go from one building to another dangling from a rope," Borden says. "It was something of an optical illusion because there was a platform below her. If she dropped, she would've dropped only six feet onto the platform. Still, she was fifty feet in the air, six flights up. It was only by angling the camera and shooting down that we got the shot. There was risk involved and Isabella handled it like a pro."

When Hackford and Borden saw the dailies, they knew they had cast a new star.

"I remember sitting in the screening room and saying, 'My God, she looks like her mother. . . . Isabella has the same haunting quality her mother had," Borden says. It doesn't come across in her Lancôme ads. But it carries on the screen. On screen, she is definitely a product of her mother. And the next thing you ask is, 'Is this an asset or a liability?' I don't think her mother could ever be a liability. There is a quality of movie star in her mother that is undeniable and that quality carries over in Isabella. In many ways, Isabella is not as beautiful in that classic way as her mother but she has all the internal beauty in her eyes."

Speaking of Isabella's other similarities to her mother, Borden adds, "She demanded presence on the screen. That is the quality of a star. The exact nature of a movie star is hard to put into words. You look at an actor like Marlon Brando and you say, 'Why is he so interesting to watch?' Then you see another actor or actress and they're very good, but they don't demand to be watched on the screen. When Isabella is on the screen, you want to watch her. It's not that you have to be beautiful. There are a lot of actors who demand to be watched, who aren't beautiful. It's an intangible quality. You can see it on film and the audience sees it on film whether they know it or not. That is the difference between a good actor and a great actor. Isabella is great."

Hackford and Borden were proud to be the ones to "break" Isabella as an American star. By the time she appeared in *Blue Velvet*, she had grown by leaps and bounds as an actress.

"You can see it in *White Nights*, Borden says, "even though the role doesn't stretch her out. In *Blue Velvet* David stretched her out more and she demanded to be watched.

"I thought she'd matured as an actress enormously and that David got a great performance out of her. She had to stretch inside and find things that probably weren't really her. She did a magnificent job. It took a lot of guts. To do what she did with the confidence she had with the emotional weight she brought to it, is not an easy thing. It's not easy clothed, much less naked."

Borden believes that Isabella came into her own only after being liberated—in a positive sense—from her past.

"I don't think Isabella's sense of direction was established before her mother died," Borden says. "Maybe she was overshadowed by both her parents. There is a saying that when a man's mother dies, it's a very sad time, but also a very liberating time for some reason. He is able to cut the tie. He can move ahead as a man when his mother is dead because he has no emotional obligations to his mother. That is a very strong tie. You always do everything for the mother, to please the mother. Once she is dead, that obligation is gone. There is sense of that with Isabella.

"I don't think Isabella's parents scared her off from the movie business but I don't think she had the direction she has now until after they were dead and she had fewer emotional ties. She looked around and said, 'Maybe this is my direction and, coincidentally, it's the same as my parents.' After her parents were dead, she felt strong enough to do whatever she wanted.

"It's a subtle difference. I think Isabella is a woman who found herself at thirty saying, 'Now what do I want to do?' and she said, 'I want to be in the movie industry.'"

There is no question that Isabella Rossellini typifies the path that every woman, with luck, travels one day—the road to independence. Her struggle to stand in her own light has been both inspiring and courageous. Bill Borden remembers a moment of great insight into Isabella. Borden happened to be at a mixing studio recently while working on *La Bamba*, which he co-produced with Taylor Hackford.

"We were dubbing the film and the same people who were mixing our picture happened to have mixed Marty Scorcese's last picture during the time when Isabella was married to him. The engineer asked me about *White Nights*. When he found out that Isabella was in it, he told me how she used to accompany Scorcese to the sound stage every day. She came nearly every day for six weeks. And he never knew her to say a word. Not one word in all that time."

She listened and she learned. And Isabella found her voice.

CHAPTER
15

NEVER CALL AN ITALIAN SMALL POTATOES

Madeleine stared at Luther, her husband. *Why wouldn't he stop yelling? He disgusted her. His eyes were set too close together. She had never noticed before what a sinister cast they gave his face. How could she have married this grotesque stranger? She closed her eyes, remembering. Tim. It was because of Tim.*

Everything was perfect until Tim forced her to go down South with him in search of a thrill. Their simple, sweet lovemaking wasn't enough for him anymore—he needed new flesh. She could still remember the smell of Big Stoop, Patty's husband. She could hear Tim and Patty making love in the guest bedroom. She tried to ignore the sound of Patty's racy breathing next door and the feel of Big Stoop's rough hands on her own breasts, but it was no use. Tim and Madeleine drove back to Provincetown the next day and Madeleine couldn't bear to look Tim in the eye. They'd lost their innocence. She knew they'd never get it back.

What was that noise? Oh yes. Luther was yelling at her. She married him after Tim broke her heart. What was he saying? She couldn't quite make out the words. Something insulting, as usual. She wished he'd stop, but he yelled even louder. What was that? She hated it when he insulted her Italian background; here he was doing it again. She stared at the gun in her hand. He saw it, too, but he kept yelling. Not for a minute did he think she'd have the nerve to pull the trigger. Small potatoes. Was that what he just said?

Madeleine tried to clear her head. Her index finger rested lightly on the trigger. She realized that Luther had just crossed the line. There was no turning back. Why hadn't she thought of this before? it was so easy. Slowly, she aimed the gun at her husband. He looked at her, unafraid, and kept yelling. She smiled. She pulled the trigger. She loved the quiet.

Didn't he know better than to call an Italian small potatoes?

The first day of shooting the 1987 film *Tough Guys Don't Dance* was unforgettable. It was a frigid day in January in Provincetown, Massachusetts, and Isabella was sitting in her "honeywagon," waiting for her call. Some stars get comfortable trailers to relax in when they're not shooting, but this project didn't have a big enough budget for all the amenities. Consequently, the stars had individual rooms in the "honeywagon"—a trailer with built-in dressing rooms, all attached, that is hauled around on location by a Mack truck.

Isabella had told Nancy King, one of the assistant directors, that she would be in her dressing room, waiting for her call. When the call never came, Isabella decided to wait at the set. She stood and walked to the door. When she opened the door she heard a shriek.

"Isabella!"

Isabella clung to the door handle and looked straight down a six-foot drop. The honeywagon driver had pulled up the steps leading to her room, thinking no one was inside.

"She could've killed herself," King recalls. "All of a sudden, I saw her open the door and I thought, 'Oh, my God! Our star!' I screamed and managed to stop her though she already had quite a bit of forward momentum. It was awful . . . everything was in slow motion. But she didn't fall. She stopped just in time. She was upset, but she never complained. She never said another word about it."

Fresh from her triumph in *Blue Velvet*, Isabella almost decided not to make *Tough Guys*, even though everyone was clamoring for her.

Norman Mailer, who wrote the script and was the director, wanted Isabella for the role of Madeleine; Menahem Golan and Yoram Globus, the top brass at Cannon Films, were also hot to sign her. They couldn't help being aware of the cachet her background would lend to the picture. Francis Ford Coppola, whose production company was working in conjunction with Cannon to produce the film, thought she was perfect. John Bailey, an award-winning cinematographer who worked on such films as *Ordinary People*, *The Big Chill*, and *Silverado*, thought she would be perfect after seeing her in *Blue Velvet*.

"I thought it was an extremely courageous, daring performance," Bailey says. "I can't think of any American

actress who would've so exposed herself. Not just physically, but spiritually. She was not well-known. She was
known in terms of her family history, but not as an actress.
For her to do such a powerful characterization with such a
strong psychic and visual image—it's like going for broke
with all the attendant chances of failure or misunderstanding from American audiences."

Mailer, like Bailey, was drawn to Isabella for the pivotal
role of Madeleine after seeing her in *Blue Velvet.* "I thought
it was the first film I'd seen in years that dared to put evil
on the screen," Mailer told Gerald Peary in "Where Tough
Guys Spend the Winter," a January 16, 1987 "The Globe
and Mail" article. "And, in large measure, it succeeded."

Bailey was struck by Isabella's courage as well as the cha-
meleonlike qualities she exhibited. "I found her to be a
changeling, not in terms of her personality, but in terms of
her look. She can look very much like her mother at
times. Other times, she has quite a different look that can
be very severe and intense. I always think of her mother as
being very wide-eyed and vulnerable. Isabella certainly has
that quality. She'll catch you off guard sometimes. You'll
be standing there talking to her and she'll make a gesture,
or the light will hit her a bit differently, and you'll see her
mother.

"I was very excited about the prospect of working with
Isabella. She has the essence of a cinema persona, a powerful, visual, nonverbal projection that I think a lot of great
European actors have. They have an ability to make the
audience move toward them, rather than the more project-
ing style that American actors tend to have where they
push out to grasp an audience.

"Isabella has the ability to make you engage. It's a quiet

strength that's very compelling. Part of it is the visual appeal. It's not necessarily beauty. It's a window they have that you want to walk up and look in. We respond strongly to actors who create an aura that invites you in."

It seemed everyone wanted Isabella for the role. Isabella, however, had to be convinced. She had a hard time envisioning herself as Madeleine. Her European—and feminist—sensibilities did not take to the brutalized, degraded, and cynical view of women Mailer painted in the script of *Tough Guys*. "I felt a little ashamed because making it I felt kind of lost, Isabella told Susan Spillman of *USA Today*. "I was not sure there was supposed to be all this cynicism and I kept fighting that." Though Norman Mailer was a literary icon—he has won the National Book Award as well as the Pulitzer Prize—and despite the fact that he directed several offbeat 16mm films in the sixties, he had never been at the helm of a real Hollywood movie with a $5 million budget.

"Norman was a celebrity," King says of his ability as a director. "Before he was a talent, now he's a celebrity. Hundreds of reporters came to the set. Not to interview the stars, but to interview him. The flow of guests and visitors was incredible. Teddy Kennedy, Jr. was there with Norman's kids. The rich and elite who passed through our set as observers was incredible. We were making a movie in a goldfish bowl at the far top of the earth in freezing weather, but they still kept coming."

It was probably Mailer's reputation that finally convinced Isabella to ignore her misgivings and take the role. *Tough Guys Don't Dance* is a hardboiled murder mystery in the *film noir* style. Mailer wanted to make a statement with *Tough Guys:* "I was trying to make a film that didn't fit into a comfortable category," he said in an interview with Joe Leydon of *The Houston Post*. "I think my film lies somewhere in a no man's land between a murder mystery, a suspense tale, a film of horror, and a comedy of manners.

"The reason I wanted it to be that way is because I think life is like that. I think we're always asking ourselves when we get into extreme situations, 'Am I in a farce or am I in a tragedy? Is this funny, or is this desperate? Am I coming to the end of my string, or is this something that's really gonna enrich me six days or six years from now?'

"It's precisely what I could call an existential situation: A situation where you can't perceive the outcome of what you're doing."

Unfortunately, when *Tough Guys* was released, Mailer's "existential situation" continued; neither moviegoers nor critics understood, or liked, the outcome of his first directing effort.

"I don't think people understood the film," King says. "No one was sure what the movie was—art or bad art. For every three minutes of film, there was one minute that was great. Some of the performances were incredible."

Literary icon that Mailer is, some people still have a difficult time understanding his raw, brutal artistic voice. Including Isabella. Even though she had done her homework—reading Mailer's novel and studying the script—she still had a difficult time injecting life into the role of Madeleine.

"Isabella had a complex, difficult role and I think she was grasping very hard to understand the vernacular," Bailey says. "Mailer created a psychic and physical landscape she was not that familiar with. She and Norman were very different people, temperamentally. Norman is a verbal character. Isabella, while articulate, is more instinctive. It was not always the easiest connection. There was a great deal of respect and admiration between them, but they have different approaches. It was difficult for Isabella to always catch the cadences."

In spite of Mailer's intentions and the aching, melancholy cinematography by John Bailey, *Tough Guys Don't Dance* was never the cinematic phenomenon everyone hoped it would become. Isabella's original instincts, as it turned out, were right. Amidst the morning-after hangovers and the Hemingway tough talk, Isabella's heroine never quite locks in. She weeps, but we're not sure why. We get a glimpse of society's heinous corruptions and its evil, money-grubbing characters, but we never get past the slick surface. Isabella's Madeleine is the only character who seems to have real (if unexplained) feelings fueled by a real conscience. Unfortunately, her character does not appear often enough in the movie to make a difference.

Part of the problem, no doubt, was in Mailer's attitude. "I get on fine directing stars from Hollywood," he claimed. ". . . the women just have to be beautiful. I'll take care of the rest."

Unfortunately, Mailer didn't take care of the rest. And the difficult shoot, as well as the strange atmosphere on the set, didn't help matters.

"Our schedule was absolutely horrible," recalls King. "Every day of filming was generally pretty grim. The weather was absolutely frigid! I wore more clothes on this shoot than the one I was on in Alaska. Not only was it cold, but the actual schedule was very tight. We'd start shooting in the day, then move to night shooting, then start back in days with no break in between. We never had enough sleep. It stayed that way for eight weeks."

In spite of a lot of friction between the actors and the director, Norman Mailer held the shoot together.

"I saw him as a robust old man," King says. "Norman was not a terror. He was not an egoist. He did not yell and scream and stomp his feet.

"He's very tough, very strong, but also very kind. He can look wild when his hair sticks out from his head but he's not at all the sort of hellraiser that people imagine."

If anything, King would have preferred a bit more hellraising.

"There needed to be more laughs while we were making it," she says. "Between the long shoot and the freezing cold weather, we had a rough time."

Remaining true to her nature and her legacy, Isabella took a risk by accepting the role—in spite of her own doubts. As a result, however, she probably learned one of the actor's cardinal rules: trust your first instincts.

Trying to save all her creative and emotional energy for the difficult role of Madeleine, Isabella was a remote presence during the filming.

"Madeleine was a character who knew how to take advantage of circumstances as they fall," King says. "She was never really involved with the manipulations surrounding her. She watched her husband from the sidelines, then just took advantage of all the murder and mayhem that came out of that without getting her hands dirty."

While filming, Isabella had trouble actually saying some of Norman's lines. She was not so startlingly "present" as she was in *Blue Velvet*.

"I think she was very unsure why she was picked for this

role and exactly what to do with it," King says. "There were times when I thought she felt awkward saying these lines."

The atmosphere on the set didn't help. "There was a strange attitude towards women on this show," King remembers.

"It was a bleak . . . movie [in terms of women]. Isabella didn't fit in and I think she felt out of place. All of Norman's female characters are vicious, mean—they embody all the worst female characteristics. Isabella, on the other hand, is always very gracious to everyone. She isn't aggressive. She didn't gossip. She remained aloof, which is something most Americans don't do. They're always digging in and she's very, very private. I don't think she was comfortable with her part. And I don't think she and Norman ever came to any kind of understanding."

Isabella played a role for which she was probably not ideally suited. In spite of that, she was good in *Tough Guys*, though not as compelling as she was in *Blue Velvet*. Norman Mailer was not able to make her feel comfortable or inspired, as David Lynch had.

King saw Isabella Rossellini as an actress, woman, and daughter, who was still finding her way and carving out her niche. "I think Isabella is sensitive to the fact that her mother was such a beautiful woman, such a well respected actress and I think she's probably still at that point where she wonders if people aren't going after her for who she is as opposed to what she can do," King says, adding, "She never spoke about her parents. She seemed to have a need within herself to present herself as she is without making any changes, without making any apologies.

"It's hard to be honest about yourself and not apologize

for who you are. When you can do it, then you can finally grow up. But there can be a lot of antagonism within yourself about doing that. I sensed that in Isabella. You're afraid of being rejected, yet you eventually come to a point where you reach success and you face yourself. Isabella seems determined to just be herself. It's something that takes tremendous courage."

And garners a great deal of respect.

Not exactly small potatoes.

CHAPTER

16

THE RISK OF
BEING A CHAMELEON

Marie clutches the knife. *The sun glints off the long steel blade. She runs toward the little stone church where her husband is having his siesta. He used to come home to her. They would lie together and watch the afternoon sun die out, whispering secrets. Until she came—The American sky diver. Augustine said she was nothing more than a daredevil. Claire-on-a-dare. He said he hated what she did. Why, then, did he seem to care so much? Marie ran faster. She would not lose her husband to this blond-haired bitch. Why did Claire fly all the way over here from America? Why now? What about her own husband? The sun was high overhead. No one played in the courtyard by the church at this hour. She didn't need to hide the knife. Maybe he's not even there. Maybe the American* went home. *That's what her husband told her. He swore it on his good name. He wouldn't lie to her . . . would he? She would find out for herself. She ran faster and faster, her sandals slapping at the earth. One, two, three she bounded the steps to the church. She threw open the door—and a wild, uncontrollable rush of animal hatred engulfed her. She screamed. The sound seemed alien, distant, too ferocious to be coming from her lips. The American bitch was here. Making love to her husband. Claire had managed to pull him into her seductive web. It was all her fault. Her husband loved her, his wife. He was a victim, a pawn. Marie moved in for the kill, like an animal, propelled by a momentum she hardly understood but knew she could not stop. Claire struggled to pull her dress on—a red dress, the dress of a whore. Marie raised her knife above her head and thrust it into the belly of the whore. She thrust the knife in again, turning the blade. Claire fell to the floor, her belly ripped open, a red gash to match her dress. Marie could hear her husband crying. She was shaking. She couldn't stop.*

The 1987 film *Siesta* is not an easy movie to categorize. Even the director, Mary Lambert, can't sum it up in one sentence. If high-concept films—those that can be described in one line—are the norm, *Siesta* is out of the mainstream.

"It's a movie about an obsession with physical passion," Lambert told John Howell of *Elle* magazine. Lambert added, "It's about death as a metaphor for positive change." "This woman is desperately in love with this man and what he represents to her—danger."

"It's about accepting and embracing change and going on to the next reality."

Mary Lambert's voice has the gentle Southern cadences

of her native Arkansas. It is a feminine voice, a soft voice, but always a passionate one. Her stunning green eyes express myriad emotions, by turns playful, serious, and intense, never bored. She made a name for herself directing music videos for such stars as Madonna, Sheila E, and Annie Lennox. Prince "discovered" her on the set of a Sheila E video and asked her to direct him in *Under the Cherry Moon*.

The young director lost no time getting the ball rolling with *Siesta*. Like Isabella, she loves taking risks. To tackle a story about sex and death that jumps around in a nonlinear fashion, is, for a first-time director, fairly awe-inspiring. Lambert was drawn to *Siesta* because she found it to be "the most unusual script [she had] ever read and the only one that was successful at existing from the point of view of the subconscious."

No one was standing in line to finance such an unusual film. Raising venture capital was a long hard struggle. In many ways, Lambert worked in reverse order; she put together her cast and crew before she secured the financing.

"I staked quite a bit of my reputation on making sure the project was going," Lambert says. She was determined to make it happen. "People were giving so much to me I hated to throw all their hard work back in their faces.

"I spent a lot of time putting together the cast and crew. . . . I had an incredible group of people—not just the cast, but the crew. They were not the kind of people who could sit around and wait for six months while I was raising money.

"We were in preproduction, we were rehearsing, and we still didn't have it. As a director you have to be many things to many people. You have to be an authority figure and you have to give people confidence in the project, but at a certain point, I didn't know if I was giving people confidence or lying to them."

Patricia Knop, the writer of *Siesta*, also wondered if her film would ever get made. Dozens of directors read the script. While a lot of them liked the material, most of them felt the approach was too original, too unique. It would never get made, they said.

"There is a constant theme in my work," Knop says, sitting at her desk in her Hollywood Hills home. "Going to the edge. I'm amazed how frightened people are of going to the edge. My husband and I wrote *9½ Weeks* and, originally, the story was very, very similar to *Siesta*. It's about someone pushing someone to the edge and the other person allowing it; the idea that you have to fall or regain your footing."

Lambert loved the script. It was precisely the fragmented narrative and dreamy surrealism other directors had shied away from that drew her to the project. "I think that's probably a fault of mine," Lambert says reflectively. "I usually bite off more than I should. Sometimes I pull it off. I'm never happy in safe territory."

The path to Hollywood was not a common one for Lambert. Arkansas born and bred, she studied at the Rhode Island School for Design in the early seventies. She worked as a painter and made several short films before directing music videos.

When Lambert couldn't raise the money to make *Siesta* in California, she traveled to London. Ellen Barkin was cast in the lead and Isabella was slated for a pivotal supporting role. The rest of the cast included Gabriel Byrne,

Julian Sands of *Room with a View*, Martin Sheen, and Jodie Foster—all of whom committed their time and energy to the film before the backers were solidly behind the project. Despite the loyalty of this impressive cast, the project almost died again two weeks before shooting, when one backer dropped out and another one had to be found—posthaste.

"*Siesta* got made because a lot of people put faith in one another," Lambert says. "Nobody made any money. Everybody worked on deferments. I knew it was a house of cards. I had my life staked. It's a stressful, scary way to do something."

Finally, Lambert raised the money and the project was a "go." Shooting began in May of 1987.

"I believe if I really want to do something the force of my own will is enough to accomplish it," Lambert says. "I have a curious ability to turn off anxiety when I have to. It's like going into battle; you can't worry about getting shot. Most people drown because they panic."

Once filming began, Lambert let go of her siege mentality and dug into the task at hand—directing. Though she said all the actors were "a joy" to work with, Lambert agrees Isabella brought special qualities to her role. Different aspects of Isabella's style and approach captivated the film's director and writer.

"I loved the sense of explosiveness under the surface with Isabella," Lambert says. "It's an amazing part of her."

"She has a great mystery about her," Knop adds. Both women agree that Isabella brought something special and rare to her role as Marie.

"Isabella comes into her own when you give her something difficult to do," Lambert says. "I think the hardest part for her, and for me as a director directing her, was having her be a restrained little wife who does whatever her husband wants her to do in the earlier scenes.

"As soon as you give her something that's out there and physical and difficult, there's no problem. She takes over. She likes the challenge of portraying an abnormal situation, or an exacerbated emotional moment. She loves that. . . . The day we shot the scene where she stabs Ellen, she was great."

Not only was Isabella great in front of the camera, she was a steady source of support to her fellow actors.

"Whenever you film a violent scene, you have to be careful," Lambert says. "Obviously, Isabella wasn't going to stick the knife in Ellen, but she did have a real knife for some of the shots. When you have a struggle like that someone can get accidentally hurt very easily, just because they're moving quickly. Ellen was naked, she didn't have any protection. She had to fall on the floor. It would've been very easy for Ellen to get a nasty scratch across her face and Isabella was really a pro about it. She calmed Ellen down.

"As soon as you give Isabella a strong emotional moment, she just goes for it. You almost have to hold her back. She loves it.

"It's so at odds with her physical exterior because she's so classically lovely and her faces exudes this kind of peace. She exudes a sense of European culture. That's her exterior, but let me tell you, inside she's a fireball. She really is. There was a big difference between the scenes that were sedentary and her character was more retiring and running away from conflict and the scenes that were more demanding. She did the tough scenes with ease."

As Lambert describes Isabella, the line between Ingrid and Isabella once again becomes blurred, as Isabella begins to manifest the professionalism her mother was known for as an actress.

"Isabella is a complete perfectionist," Lambert says. "If something's not right, she won't go for it. If she doesn't feel it, she won't live with it, or tolerate it. She won't accept something that's not quite there.

"She really wants direction from a director. She wants direction and she wants explanation. She wants to know what does this mean and why do you think that? What do I do now and why are you changing it? She really challenges you as a director to put up or shut up."

Lambert is known as a director who respects her actors and treats them as artists. She does not believe in manipulating or trying to trick them into creating certain emotional moments. "I don't think you have to fool people into giving a good performance." she says. "I like to have more of a rapport between me and the actor so we're all working towards the same goal. I don't think humiliation should be used as a tool. The important thing is to set really high standards and not accept anything that falls beneath those standards. *Siesta* was very difficult to direct because the emotions and the characters are not very straightforward."

"Thank God for Isabella," she continues. "Her emotions were a little more straightforward. Basically, her character is just as passionate as Ellen's character. We just had to find a way for her to show that in an intense and believable way, a way that fit in with her character.

"Sometimes as a director you can help with a very visual or technical direction, like 'Don't move your hands when you say that line' or 'Put equal emphasis on each word.'

"I couldn't work with Isabella that way. She wanted to understand why she was doing things. She wanted an emotional response for her actions because she felt, quite rightly, her character had to be very emotional to commit a murder. She was right. She wasn't going to let me get away with anything. Not that I wanted to! But with her character it was impossible to say 'Speak in a monotone and don't wiggle.' She needed a reason and we spent a lot of time working those reasons out.

"We shot the scene in the cafe with more takes than we did on anything else in the movie. . . . That's the point where she decides to kill Ellen. . . . Isabella decides, if this lady screws around with my husband, I'm going to kill her. It's a quiet decision, but it's a very passionate decision. We had a real hard time getting that scene right because it was so important. It had to be uncomfortable. A man who is faced with his wife and his mistress, and his mistress is confronting him in front of his wife, is [in] an uncomfortable scene. That's not a scene most men will run to. I didn't want to seem too witty as if this is how adults have fun. It wasn't that kind of movie. It wasn't a Beverly Hills farce."

Lambert, too, is a perfectionist. They shot the scene until they got it right. The crew got an extra long lunch break while the director and the actress worked on her character's motivation.

"We tried the scene over and over again and we finally got it. At the end, when Isabella stabs Ellen with the knife, it was funny to me to see Isabella come to life. The scene you'd think would be difficult—struggling with the knife and the naked man—was easy for her. She loved it. She was great. The more out there it is, the more naturally she comes to it.

"To be able to lose restraint like that is very difficult. There are two difficult things for an actor—to be able to show something with great restraint and to be able to show something with no restraint. Those are the two extremes and that's what Isabella had to do in *Siesta*. She didn't have any easy scenes where she could just walk through them. I see someone who is struggling to be the best actress she can be, someone trying to challenge boredom."

A great actor projects different things to different people—without even trying. Patricia Knop experienced Isabella primarily as a woman of mystery. Both women agree that Isabella is a woman of passion.

"We offered *Siesta* to Isabella and I was amazed when she said she would do it," Knop says. "She's great in it. No, amazing in it.

"I really believe that she is one of our great actresses. I think she's got great mystery. That's why she is able to step in and play a killer and we can believe it with that beautiful angel face. She's got such power and hidden mystery about her. There are a lot of beautiful faces out there, but she's special and she's got tremendous warmth."

Perhaps Knop's favorite part of the European shoot was the time she spent with Isabella away from the set. Knop gained great insight into Isabella's European roots when she visited her in Barcelona. While making *Siesta*, Isabella stayed with Miguel Bose, a childhood friend who had grown up to be a European pop star.

"Miguel's house is totally filled with Picasso's work," Knop says. "Picasso used to do great big life-sized figures and lay them in bed with the children so that they wouldn't feel all alone. These incredible Picasso figures are now framed in their bedrooms.

"Everything was rambling and completely white, with

emerald green lawns with ten big white dogs romping across the lawn.

"Isabella was all in white. The setting captured the essence of her European mystery. There is an amazing glamor to her, an untouchable amazing quality to her.

"You think of her past and the things she's seen and the way in which she's grown up and it's incredible. Everywhere we went in Europe—Italy, all over, her face was everywhere. Giant posters with her face staring out were in every cosmetic store."

As an actress, Isabella was all that Patricia could have hoped for—and then some.

"Isabella is one of the few actresses I've met who's incredibly willing to go to the edge every single time. Marie is not an attractive role and yet I'm sure she took it because of the fact that's its amazingly out here. When you only see Isabella for a few moments in the film and for most of that time she's brutally killing someone, it's not terribly sympathetic.

"That is where the power lies with Isabella. There was an entire block filled with mothers and daughters the day Mary shot the church scene. Isabella was a pro.

"I think she's courageous. Her spirit is so expansive. She has such an ability to laugh and ride the waves. In person, she is not guarded. She is extraordinarily giving in a way that is doubly unusual."

Though David Lynch was not present during the shoot, Knop felt his influence in the material.

"I think there are some things in common between *Siesta* and *Blue Velvet*." she said. "They both try to break the mold. Both of them achieve that. They aren't formula films. I think it's a miracle both of those films got made."

After spending some time with Isabella and Lynch,

Knop found them to be well suited personally as well as artistically.

"They seem perfect for each other," Knop says. "They're incredibly loving and wonderful. Really, really wonderful."

Knop finds great comfort in the fact that David Lynch has created something of a mainstream career while maintaining his artistic vision.

Knop is following in Lynch's footsteps. Though *Siesta* was launched in only a few theaters, word of mouth has kept moviegoers coming. Knop couldn't be more pleased.

"I love the film," she says. "I haven't really looked at the reviews. It sounds jaded, but I really don't care. My husband came in with the *Los Angeles Times* and he was so worried and I didn't care. I feel such pride in the fact that the film was done and was done according to my vision. When I look at it, it looks perfect. I get an incredible rush of emotion everytime I see it."

Both Patricia Knop and Mary Lambert want to work with Isabella again. Both feel that Isabella is finally standing in her own light as an actress. Neither sees her as struggling with her complicated legacy. If anything, she seems like a woman who has resolved her past, taken all the riches it has to offer and used them to build her own life. Patricia remembers that at one point during the shooting of *Siesta*, Isabella was considering a remake of *Anastasia*, one of her mother's films.

"She thought it would be really interesting to do something her mother had done, but to do it in her own way," Patricia recalls.

Isabella seems to have emerged from the shadows. By embracing her parents' legacy, she has gone beyond it, a passage that has defined her as a woman, a mother, and an actress. By going to the edge, she has stepped into the light.

CHAPTER

17

STANDING IN THE LIGHT

Zelly took Phoebe in her arms. Coco watched her every move, but Zelly refused to succumb to Coco's malevolent gaze. Zelly loved Phoebe as if she were her own child. And what a child she was. Just a second ago, Phoebe had stood up to the police and to Coco, telling them that she, Zelly, hadn't tried to kidnap her. Just the opposite was true. Zelly desperately wanted to take Phoebe away to Europe, away from Coco, who was crushing Phoebe's spirit. But she couldn't do it alone and Willy had lied to her.

Zelly gently stroked Phoebe's cheek, thinking of what her bravery would cost her. Coco would make Phoebe's life miserable for this show of independence. She would destroy Phoebe's most precious possessions, her stuffed animals. Zelly shuddered, pulling the child close. She spoke to Phoebe, the daughter she never had, the child she had mothered for so long. "No matter what happens," she told her, "I will always love you . . . and we will always be together." Zelly could feel Phoebe clinging to the words, knowing, with a child's wisdom, what lay ahead. Always, she would treasure Zelly's words. They would live inside her heart, like a precious jewel to light up her soul whenever Coco hurt her—as Phoebe knew she would, again and again. Kneeling at Phoebe's feet, Zelly said good-bye. For the rest of Zelly's life, Phoebe, the child she could not save, would live in her heart.

Isabella is, unequivocally, in full possession of her powers as an actress. She fills every frame of *Zelly and Me,* Tina Rathborne's story released in 1988 of what happens to a gifted young child when love is withdrawn and acts of cruelty are visited upon her.

"From the very beginning there was never anyone else for the role of Zelly," says Sue Jett, who, with her partner Tony Mark, produced Rathborne's first feature film under the powerful wing of David Puttnam, who gave the project the green light while still running the show at Columbia as chairman and chief executive officer.

When Jett met Isabella, she was impressed by one quality in particular. "The thing that struck me the most about Isabella is that she is very unafraid to look at life. She has a way of facing what reality is. There's no extraneous surface quality about her. There is not much chitchat. She is the kind of person who immediately delves into the issue at hand."

It was Isabella's portrayal of Dorothy Vallens in *Blue Velvet* that convinced Rathborne she was perfect for the role.

"When she clasps the child to her breast [in the last

scene of *Blue Velvet*], she has this look of maternal rapture in her eyes," Rathborne said. "I saw that last shot and I thought, 'There is Zelly.'"

At the time, Rathborne was still working on the script but she couldn't get Isabella out of her mind.

"It so happens that Isabella's apartment in New York is just opposite the subway stop near where I live," Rathborne said. "And having to walk by her house every day, I couldn't forget her. I couldn't say, 'Oh well, it couldn't happen.' It literally kept her in front of my eyes."

It was David Puttnam, champion of independent producers and filmmakers, who turned *Zelly and Me* into a viable project.

"It was a fairy tale," Rathborne adds. "I was sitting at my desk in New York and he called me from a pay phone in Los Angeles. I met him in New York and he gave me a ticket to the coast. I felt as though I'd tripped and fallen into another world where things magically went the way you'd hoped they would."

Once Puttnam gave *Zelly and Me* the go ahead, Sue Jett and Tony Mark came on board. Both are former New Yorkers who produced numerous "American Playhouse" productions for public television, including Rathborne's first project, "The Joy That Kills."

Isabella and Sue Jett had one thing in common—after reading the script, they both wanted to make the movie.

"I called Tina in New York," Jett recalls. "And I told her the story was so incredibly important and upsetting and complex. I told her it was a difficult movie, but one we absolutely had to make. David Puttnam was key. He encouraged an incredible blossoming of talent."

Preproduction lasted for several months. During this

stage, Isabella played an unusual role for any actress, but especially for the star of the picture.

"She put in a tremendous amount of time and energy into the casting process in order to help get the elements right," Jett says. "And that is very, very rare."

Finally, all the roles were cast. Glynis Johns was Coco, Phoebe's abusive grandmother, who was starved for love herself; Alexandra Johnes was Phoebe; John Heard was set to play Willy; Joe Morton was to be Earl; and Kaiulani Lee as the maid.

Tina was ready to begin shooting—until she realized she had a director's nightmare on her hands. There was simply no chemistry between Isabella and John Heard.

"We hired John and he's a marvelous actor," Jett said. "He and Isabella rehearsed together, but it just wasn't working. We agonized and Isabella agonized but they weren't able to play against each other and time was running out."

At this point, Isabella suggested what has since been deemed a stroke of genius. Why not audition David Lynch for the role of Willy?

"We had very narrow minds," Jett says with a laugh. "And we thought, 'David Lynch? A director?' And we said, 'No. No. No. We need someone who acts.'"

It was a difficult role to cast. "Willy is not your Don Johnson kind of guy," Jett explained. "And he's not so great. He doesn't save the woman. He doesn't come through. He's a man who doesn't have his own life. He's stunted emotionally. Very few actors wanted to play him."

Isabella did not give up. She asked Tina and Sue if David could come in so that they could tape a scene together. Director and producer relented and the proof was in the tape.

"Isabella shimmered across from David," Jett says. "She blossomed. When we saw how she came alive with David, this loveliness she exuded, we called Columbia and said, 'This man is Willy.'

"You can't hide chemistry. There is a special quality you see on the screen when two people love each other. You can't hide it from the camera."

Rathborne felt blessed as a director. "When I met David, he had that wryness and that sweetness and the manliness and he's very handsome, but at the same time, he's other-worldly. He had all the qualities I wanted."

Just as she became Dorothy Vallens in *Blue Velvet*, Isabella inhabits the role of Zelly, a woman Jett describes as "a bit of a spinster who needs love and who has interjected herself in a family in an almost unhealthy way."

There is nothing like the validation of one's peers. Joe Morton, an actor's actor who has appeared in various roles at New York's prestigious Public Theater and is also known for his starring role in John Sayles' film *The Brother From Another Planet*, gives Isabella high marks.

"I'd seen *Blue Velvet* and I was very curious about her," Morton commented. "When someone does something like the work she did in that film, you're not sure if that's a one-shot deal. She's a wonderful actress and she's exceptional in *Zelly and Me*.

"She always came to the set prepared. She'd done her homework and she had a point of view on her character and she was willing to give and take. She doesn't simply say 'This is what I'm going to do and now what are you going to do?' She gives you as much off camera as she does on camera. She's a real partner when you play a scene opposite her. She's not just there for her takes and her closeups. She's working with you in conjunction and not off on her own. That's what makes a good actor. Someone who is willing to share. She's also very generous. Isabella never played star. She was just a normal human being doing a movie with the rest of us."

Jett offers an explanation of Isabella's accessible nature. "She is an extraordinarily courageous woman and she has a tremendous ability to be in the moment. To do that, you have to be in touch with who you are and that takes the courage of introspection. She's looked inside and faced what's there and she's comfortable with what she's found.

"She's really willing to participate in life, whether it's playing with a puppy that strays onto the set or working with a child actress, she embraces life. It's a wonderful and rare quality."

That ability to immerse oneself in life is doubly difficult for a star, Jett believes. "Stars are constantly in the public eye and they can build up an artificial persona to deal with it. Isabella has none of that."

Tina Rathborne came to know Isabella in a relatively short time. To create the magic they wanted on screen, both women chose to dispense with social formalities and get to know each other quickly. *Zelly and Me* was the start of a friendship between them. They discussed their lives, their pasts, and discovered they shared many of the same childhood experiences.

"We talked a lot about growth," Rathborne said. "It fascinates both of us. I think that's why Isabella seemed to genuinely love my story about a child maintaining her identity in the face of withdrawal of love and cruel acts of fate. *Zelly and Me* is about the voyage of an identity.

"Isabella and I have talked about her voyage and how far she's come. But that is what life is all about. We are all identities in the making."

Isabella has arrived. She stands squarely in her own light, poised and ready for her future.

EPILOGUE

sabella had a difficult time stepping from the long shadows cast by the love and legacy of her parents. "I have
had identity problems all my life," she said in a March
10, 1986 issue of *People* magazine. Through much of
her twenties and, to some extent, her early thirties, Isabella has tried to find her way. It has been a long process,
but each foray, professional and personal, has given her
a little more strength, a little more confidence. When
her father and then her mother passed away, she was prepared at last to assume control of her own life, like a
thoroughbred heading into a race. Isabella has been a success in everything she has attempted. She is the highest-
paid model in the United States, with a record-setting contract with Lancôme. She wasn't an overnight sensation
with films, for acting is an art that is not mastered overnight.

Unlike her mother's films, each of which was a box-
office smash prior to Ingrid's fall from grace, only a few of
Isabella's films have reached that Hollywood state of grace.
But true artists do not choose films based on their box-
office potential. To say something, to move the audience,
to move society forward—these are their motivations. So
it wasn't until Isabella made the controversial *Blue Velvet*
with David Lynch that she could, perhaps, look in the
mirror and say, "I am an artist." Just like her father, a man
who was inspired by the same artistic endeavors.

Tall, dark, and possessing an unusual beauty, Isabella Rossellini is, in many respects, like her mother. In other respects, moved to explore the darker side of life on film, she is very much her father's daughter. When Ingrid and Roberto married, they spent many years making movies that attempted to do more than create a cash flow for the producers. They attempted art. They tried to tell the truth about aspects of the human condition. The public rejected their attempts.

Today, looking at their daughter, one realizes that Isabella Rossellini is her own person, but she is also the undeniable sum of her parents, their genes, their minds. Above all, Isabella is an artist, doing exactly what her parents tried to do with their films. She is living out a version of their vision and values.

Ingrid Bergman and Roberto Rossellini's daughter is a success.

BIBLIOGRAPHY

Adams, Scott. *"Blue Velvet."* *Movieline,* September 1986, 12, 13.

Ansen, David. "Rossellini's *Renaissance."* *Newsweek,* May 21, 1979, 67.

————."Hoofing It to Freedom." *Newsweek,* November 1985, 94.

————. "Stranger Than Paradise." *Newsweek,* September 15, 1986, 67.

Bailey, John (Visual consultant, *Tough Guys Don't Dance*). Personal interview, December 15, 1987.

Battelle, Phyllis. "Isabella Rossellini: Like Mother, Like Daughter?" *Ladies Home Journal,* November 1985, 97, 98, 208–209.

Bergman, Ingrid, and Alan Burgess. *My Story.* New York: Dell Publishing, 1985.

Borden, Bill (Producer, *White Nights*). Personal interview, December 10, 1987.

Bordon, Lizzie. "The World According to Lynch." *Village Voice,* September 3, 1986, 62, 66.

Brady, James. "In Step with Isabella Rossellini." *Parade*, October 5, 1986, 30.

Byrne, Bridget. "Matter of Time." *Los Angeles Herald-Examiner*, October 8, 1976, B-3.

Canby, Vincent. "Roberto Rossellini Lets Reality Speak for Itself." *New York Times*, June 19, 1977, D-170.

———. "Screen: *The Meadow* from Italy." *New York Times*, May 7, 1982, C-8.

———. "Film: Baryshnikov in *White Nights*, Tale of Two Defectors." *New York Times*, November 22, 1985, C-10.

———. "Film: Norman Mailer's *Tough Guys Don't Dance*." *New York Times*, September 18, 1987, C-14.

Carr, Jay. "*Blue Velvet* Already a Classic." *Boston Globe*, April 12, 1987, 15.

Champlin, Charles. "Ingrid Bergman: A Triumph of Time." *Los Angeles Times*, March 18, 1979, page 1, Calendar Section.

———. "Rossellini Shines on Her Own in *White Nights*." *Los Angeles Times*, November 14, 1985, 1, 17.

Chase, Donald. "Isabella Rossellini Makes a Smooth Turn in *Velvet*," *USA Today*, October 24, 1986, 4-D.

Chute, David. "Mother Nature as Seductress." *Los Angeles Herald-Examiner*, January 12, 1983, C-2.

Clark, Mike. "*White Nights* Fades Out Quickly." *USA Today*, November 11, 1985, 6D.

———. "A Strange and Original 'Blue Velvet.'" *USA Today*, September 19, 1986, 5-D.

Cook, Bruce. "Isabella Rossellini: A Rose Who Has Known Thorns." *Chicago Tribune*, November 28, 1985, 14V.

Corliss, Richard. "It's a Strange World, Isn't It?" *Time*, September 22, 1986, 86.

Darn, Nina. "At the Movies." *New York Times*, September 1, 1987, C-10.

Denby, David. "Flesh and Fantasy." *New York*, September 29, 1986, 85, 86.

Ebert, Roger. "Norman Mailer, the Director." *New York Post*, December 26, 1986, 33, 34.

―――. "Isabella Rossellini Follows the Trail Her Parents Blazed." *Chicago Sun-Times*, May 17, 1987, 2, Show Section.

Eisenberg, Lawrence. "Bella Bella Isabella." *Cosmopolitan*, February, 1983, 68, 69, 72, 73, 77.

Feeny, F. X. "*The Meadow* Pick of the Week." *L. A. Weekly*, January 7, 1983, 12-14.

Fink, Mitchell. "Get Me Re-write." *Los Angeles Herald-Examiner*, August 27, 1987, A-2.

Gelmis, Joseph. "A Child of the Movies Makes Movie." *Los Angeles Times*, May 23, 1982, 27.

―――. "Norman Mailer's Mayhem on Cape Cod." *San Francisco Chronicle*, January 18, 1987, 19, 20.

Gooch, Brad. "Will Flick Click?" *Vanity Fair*, November, 1987, 54, 58, 60, 62–64, 66.

Healey, Michael. "Mailer Mystery Deceiving Gem." *Los Angeles Daily News*, September 20, 1987, 15.

Hedman, Stan. "Ingrid Bergman's Daughter Is Here Looking at You." *Sunday Woman*, September 2, 1979, 8, 9.

Hess, John. "Roberto Rossellini, Director, Dies, Master of Postwar Film Realism." *New York Times*, June 4, 1977, 22.

Hoberman, J. "Return to Normalcy." *Village Voice*, September 23, 1986, 58.

Hotchner, A. E. "The Enduring Courage of Ingrid Bergman." *McCall's*, May, 1982, 85, 86, 156, 158, 162.

Howell, John. "Virgin Moviemaker, Mary Lambert." *Elle*, August, 1987, 48.

Hutchings, David. "People: Isabella Rossellini." *People*, October 21, 1986, 45.

————. "Here's Looking at You, Kid: Ingrid Bergman's Daughter Isabella May Be the New Star in the Family." *People*, August 2, 1982, 91, 92.

"Isabella, Bergman's Daughter, Bids for Stardom." *Life*, November, 1985, 135, 136, 140.

"Isabella as Mom Ingrid on TV." *USA Today*, May 12, 1985, C-1.

Israel, Frank. "Optical Illusions." *GQ*, April, 1982, 24, 25.

"Italo Strikes, Holidays, Mixups, A Matter of Time for the Minellis." *Variety*, February 4, 1976, 30.

Jaehne, Karen. "Mailer's Minuet." *Film Comment*, December, 1987, 11–17.

Jett, Sue (Producer, *Zelly and Me*). Personal interview, January 11, 1988.

Kael, Pauline. *"A Matter of Time."* *The New Yorker*, February, 1976, 36–38.

———. *"The Current Cinema."* *The New Yorker*, September 22, 1986, 99, 100–103.

Kilday, Greg. "A Stand on *A Matter of Time.*" *Los Angeles Times*, October 16, 1976, 15.

King, Nancy (Assistant director, *Tough Guys Don't Dance*). Personal interview, December 13, 1987.

Klemesrud, Judy. "Ingrid Bergman: No Regrets at 65." *New York Times*, October 7, 1980, C-1.

Knop, Patricia (Writer, *Siesta*). Personal interview, January 20, 1988.

Kunk, Deborah J. *"Tough Guys* Doesn't Have What It Takes." *Los Angeles Herald-Examiner*, September 18, 1987, 8.

Lally, Kevin. *"White Nights* Unites Two Dance Worlds." *Film Journal*, June 1985, 12, 74.

Lambert, Mary. (Director, *Siesta*). Personal interview, January 15, 1988.

"A Lapse of Memory." *Time*, November 8, 1976, 63.

Leamer, Laurence. *As Time Goes By*, New York: Harper & Row, 1986.

"Lynch Break." *Details*, October 1986, 38, 39.

Mallory, Carole Wagner. "Intermezzo with Isabella." *New Woman*, October 1987, 65, 67, 68.

Mann, Roderick. "Papa et Fille, Finally Get It Together." *Los Angeles Times*, February 8, 1976, 15, 16.

Maslin, Janet. "Screen: *Blue Velvet*, Comedy of the Eccentric." *New York Times*, September 19, 1986, C-2.

———. "Film Exoticism in *Siesta*." *New York Times*, November 11, 1987, C-23.

Mathews, Jack. "David Lynch Stares Down Life's Dark Side." *Los Angeles Times*, September 26, 1986, 22.

"A Matter of Time." The New Yorker, November 1, 1976, 85.

"A Matter of Time." Village Voice, November 8, 1976, 42.

McGuigan, Cathleen. "Black and Blue Is Beautiful?" *Newsweek*, October 27, 1986, 102, 104.

Metzner, Sheila. "The Essence of Change." *Vogue*, May 1986, 329.

Mitchell, Sean. "Delving into the Dark Side of *Blue Velvet's* David Lynch." *Los Angeles Herald-Examiner*, September 16, 1986, D-1, D-5.

Morton, Joe (Co-star in *Zelly and Me*). Personal interview, December 8, 1988.

"Mum's the Word." *Vanity Fair*, January 1985, 57.

Napoli, Toni. "*The Meadow*." *Film Journal*, March 22, 1982, 21.

Paul, Jacob. "Rossellini: Intrepid Italian." *Movieline*, September 12, 1986, 13, 14.

Peary, Gerald. "Where Tough Guys Spend the Winter." *The Globe and Mail*, January 16, 1987, D-3, D-4.

Powers, John. "Bleak Chic." *American Film*, March 1987, 47–51.

————. "Hollywood's Babylon." *L. A. Weekly*, July 24, 1987, 43, 44.

Prebula, Greg J. *"A Matter of Time." Hollywood Reporter*, October 6, 1976, 3.

Previn, Steve (Producer, *A Matter of Time*). Personal interview, November 16, 1987.

Rathborne, Tina (Writer-director, *Zelly and Me*). Personal interview, January 21, 1988.

Robertson, Nan. "The All-American Boy Behind *Blue Velvet." New York Times*, October 11, 1986, I-11.

Ryweck, Charles. *"The Meadow." Hollywood Reporter*, March 22, 1982, 3.

Sanborn, Curt. "The Eyes of Mary Lambert." *Life*, May 1986, 85-90.

Sarris, Andrew. "Random Notes on Rossellini and Other Current Concerns." *Village Voice*, June 20, 1977, 49.

Schickel, Richard. "The Price of Redemption." *Time*, September 13, 1982, 82.

Schiff, Stephen. "The Weird Dreams of David Lynch." *Vanity Fair*, March 1987, 86–90, 154, 155.

Schumach, Murray. "Ingrid Bergman, Winner of 3 Oscars, Is Dead." *New York Times*, August 31, 1982, A-1.

Shearer, Lloyd. "The Minellis Together." *Parade*, June 20, 1976, 16.

"Siesta." Variety, October 21, 1987, 3.

Skow, John. "A Model Woman, She Gets $9,000 a Day." *Time*, May 2, 1983, 50, 51.

Slatin, Judy. "A Tale of Two Brothers." *Screen International,* February, 1979, 11.

Smith, Dinitia. "Tough Guys Make Movie." *New York,* January 12, 1987, 32–35, 37.

Spillman, Susan. "Isabella's Tough Life on Film." *USA Today,* September 28, 1987, 5-D.

Standora, Leo. "Bergman Family Swamped with Cards and Letters." *New York Post,* September 2, 1982, 7, 27.

Steinbach, Alice. "On Her Own." *Saturday Review,* November 1985, 24, 26, 27, 90.

Sterritt, David. "Novelist Mailer Turns His Latest Book into Movie." *Christian Science Monitor,* September 4, 1987, 19.

Syse, Glenna. "Ingrid Bergman." *Chicago Sun-Times,* October 12, 1980, 1, Show Section.

Thomas, Kevin. "Liza's First Film for Her Father." *Los Angeles Times,* October 8, 1976, 22.

————. "Italian *Meadow* Is Fallow Ground." *Los Angeles Times,* January 12, 1983, Part VI, 1.

Thomases, Martha, and John Robert Tebbel. "Norman Makes a Movie." *New York Daily News,* February 8, 1987, 3.

Thompson, Anne. "Mary Lambert's *Siesta.*" *Movieline,* November 6, 1987, 21.

"*Tough Guys Dance.*" *Variety,* May 18, 1987, 8.

Turan, Kenneth. "Master of the Casually Grotesque." *GQ,* October 1986, 121, 124.

"*White Nights.*" *Variety,* November 6, 1985, 2.

Williams, Jeannie. "Mailer Hangs Tough Despite the Critics." *USA Today*, May 18, 1987, 70.

Wilmington, Michael. "Mailer's *Tough Guys Don't Dance*." *Los Angeles Times*, September 17, 1987, 1, 15.

Winer, Laurie. "Isabella Rossellini Assesses the Role That Haunted Her." *New York Times*, November 23, 1986, II-1.

Witchel, Alexandra. "Making It Click." *Elle*, January 1986, 29.

Wolf, William. "Heiress of Greatness." *New York*, August 9, 1982, 44, 45.

"The Year in Movies." *Rolling Stone*, November, 1986, 11.

INDEX